GETTING
THE SHOW ON

GETTING THE SHOW ON

The Complete Guidebook for Producing a Musical in Your Theater

Lehman Engel

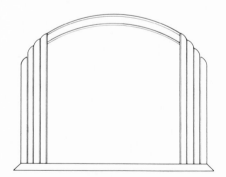

SCHIRMER BOOKS

A Division of Macmillan Publishing Co., Inc.

NEW YORK

Collier Macmillan Publishers

LONDON

Copyright © 1983 by   Schirmer Books
A Division of Macmillan Publishing Co., Inc.

226254

Schirmer Books
A Division of Macmillan Publishing Co., Inc.
866 Third Avenue, New York, N.Y. 10022

Collier Macmillan Canada, Inc.

Library of Congress Catalog Card Number: 82–21603

Printed in the United States of America

printing number

1   2   3   4   5   6   7   8   9   10

Library of Congress Cataloging in Publication Data

Engel, Lehman, 1910–1982
  Getting the show on.

  Bibliography: p.
  Includes index.
  1. Musical revue, comedy, etc.—Production and
direction.   I. Title.
MT955.E55 1983   782.81′07   82–21603
ISBN 0-02-870680-3

To Jim Cavanaugh

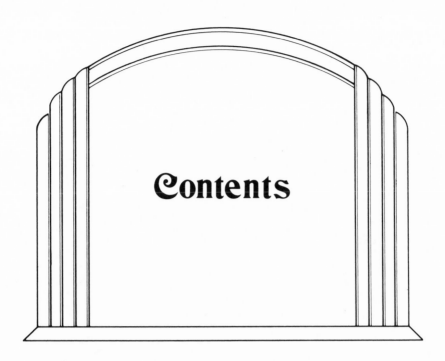

Contents

Contents

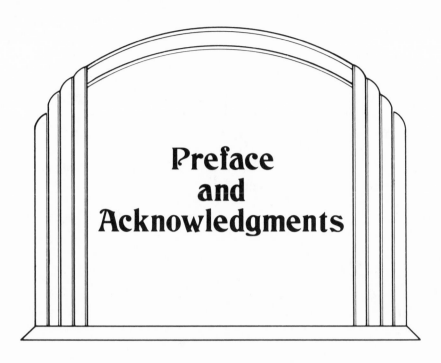

Preface
and
Acknowledgments

THE PRESENT BOOK has had an unusual history for at least two reasons.

First, this is the only one of eight books I have written that was requested: Ken Stuart, at that time editor for Schirmer Books, suggested the idea to me.

Second, the original manuscript, written during 1978 and 1979, was lost when my luggage disappeared with a "Sky Cap" (who was, in every likelihood, *not* a Sky Cap at all) in Miami. I wish this experience were unique among writers. Alas! I know that it is not. During the ensuing year and a half, I wrote the book again. Without question, it was a much better book. But that was not to be the end.

Because he wanted this to be the most useful work on the subject, Ken Stuart asked my permission to solicit some opinions. He sent the rewritten manuscript to, among others, Jim

Cavanaugh, associate professor in the Department of Theatre Arts at Mount Holyoke College in Massachusetts. Mr. Cavanaugh responded with a critique of 20 single-spaced typewritten pages. I agreed with 90 percent of his criticism and *all* of his favorable comments! I cannot thank him enough for his perceptive analysis. The only way I can hope to repay his invaluable helpfulness is to dedicate this book to him, a pleasure with which I indulge myself.

NEW YORK, 1982

Publisher's Note

On August 29, 1982, Lehman Engel died at his home in Manhattan. As editorial work on the manuscript had not been completed, we called in Jim Cavanaugh to work on and resolve myriad details concerning the book. We would like to express our gratitude to him for helping us bring it to publication.

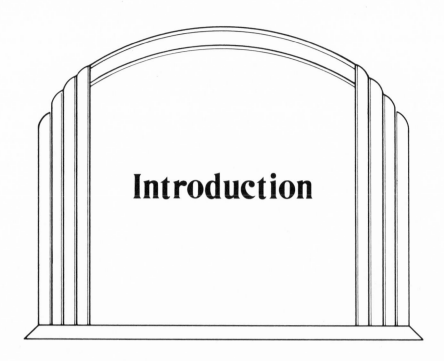

Introduction

THEATER AND MUSICAL THEATER in all their aspects generate people who may eventually become experts in their occupations if they do not attempt to start careers without both education and experience. Acting, singing, dancing, and art can be taught. The actor, singer, and dancer will never stop "taking class," even if he* dances with the American Ballet Theater, acts under Kazan, or sings at the Metropolitan Opera. All of them continue to need help, and that must be administered on a personal basis with a knowledgeable, observing "mirror" that points out errors.

*The masculine gender used throughout the book has been chosen simply to obviate the "he/she" and "his or her" awkwardness that can often arise in attempts to avoid sexist language. Unless otherwise specified, both males and females are implied in every instance; nowhere is it intended to exclude females from discussion.

Those who would study scene building, painting, costume design, and lighting design learn basic elements of their crafts in schools. But the *important* learning comes during apprenticeship. Apprenticeship is the key word. It applies to musical conductors and to those who would build anything, whether it is scenery or bridges.

Although this is, in a sense, a "how-to" book, it does not attempt to detail the building and painting of scenery or the designing and making of costumes. Separate books on these crafts are plentiful and the present author does not pretend to know anything technical about them. He is, however, experienced at first hand through decades of experience in musical theater, through close observation of the workers in all other departments, and through active collaboration in the production of 170 shows, operas, and films. His hope is that this experience can be translated here into words so that this book can be of help to others who have been less familiar with organized musical theater production.

In America during the past 40 years, productions of musical shows—mostly revivals—have skyrocketed in number. By 1971, 250 *summer* theaters performed musical shows, ranging from one to twelve shows each summer.

An increasing number of colleges, universities, and conservatories have grown more realistic during the past decade and have included musical theater alongside (and not below) their opera departments.

According to the Central Opera Service of the Metropolitan Opera, there were 77 opera-producing organizations and 13 colleges with opera workshops in the 1940–41 season. However, in 1976–77, "There were 7,389 performances of 427 operas given by a total of 914 organizations"!

It is said that the year *My Fair Lady* became available to stock and nonprofessional companies, there were more than 10,000 productions! Today, 35 years after its premiere, *Oklahoma!* is said to lead all other shows in number of regional productions, and it has once again been a hit on Broadway.

Despite television, radio, and films, this general need to perform and the real desire on the part of audiences to witness live productions demonstrate beyond any doubt the vitality of our musical theater.

These many productions have taken place under widely different and always difficult conditions. However, it is possible to create order out of chaos, to make easier what was difficult, if those who are eager to achieve a more "professional" approach to their already difficult chores will think carefully about the organization of producing, based on the evolution of professional procedures spelled out in the following pages.

Chapter 1

Producer and Staff

THERE ARE MANY ADVANTAGES that even the smallest non-professional theater enjoys over any Broadway theater. First, the initial production of a show on Broadway very often begins with an imperfect, unworkable script and score. If this particular show is to achieve any success, it requires vast libretto rewrites, deletion of and creation of new songs, trimming of dance sequences, reorchestration, and correction of many other problems. Generally, the re-creation of a show that has been revised many times during its original production does not have to be concerned with any of these problems. This is a distinct advantage that the nonprofessional producers should be grateful for.

The initial production is extremely costly because of union requirements and the many changes alluded to before.

However, there are similarities between the two kinds of

productions which should be carefully considered. Each has its own casting and rehearsal problems; each has to be carefully planned as to schedule, cost, style of production, and setting up of a staff. The end result for both Broadway and the smallest nonprofessional theater will depend in one way or another upon how well this staff works together.

Harold Prince, one of the most successful producers and directors of musical shows, once said that George Abbott had taught him to delegate authority to qualified personnel at work on a production.

This is a most important lesson for people involved in production to learn. Musical theater is the most highly collaborative of all forms, involving at the top at least a dozen people, each of whom heads, supervises, and directs the work of many others.

Whether the production of a show is for a regional theater program, a school, or Broadway, there must be a producer. He alone, or with the advice of others, chooses the show to be undertaken. He selects (sometimes with advice)—one by one—each member of the staff whose artistic job it is to provide a particular element to the production.

We might say that the production staff is divided into two parts: the operative and the creative.

The operative staff can attend to its assignments without special regard to the needs of the specific show. This portion of the staff consists first of a general manager who will, based on his previous experience, define two budgets: production and operating. Without these figures (to be detailed later), the producer is in no position to determine what his show will cost to put on the stage and to run.

Next, there should be a stage director and a production stage manager who will work under and with the stage director. In effect, the production stage manager keeps careful note of the director's orders given to the actors during rehearsals and executes the orders of the director during performances.

While each of these positions is customary and sorely needed on Broadway, what is to be accomplished by both may be taken care of in the nonprofessional theater, if necessary, by dividing the responsibilities in different ways and, in so doing, perhaps telescoping and eliminating some of the positions.

Without identifying the staff members by name (as above), let us say that for the most successful operation, the producer requires someone to create a budget based on the needs or style of the production. It is possible that this same person can also undertake the job of company manager, that is, the person who attends to the needs of the cast and staff. The separation of this job into two jobs on Broadway rests in the fact that the general manager continues working with the producer on other projected productions even while the current show is in rehearsal, while the company manager is the producer's representative with only the one show to take care of. This division is certainly unnecessary in the nonprofessional theater, where only a single show will be in production at any given time.

Similarly, stage management on Broadway is usually divided among the production stage manager, the stage manager (who is responsible for the actual day-to-day operation of the show in performance), and one or two assistant stage managers who can represent him in different parts of the backstage area during performances, and attend to demands during rehearsals that would otherwise require the production stage manager to leave the director's side. There is no reason why, with one or two dependable assistants, the production stage manager and stage manager cannot be one person; in fact, this is frequently the case even on Broadway.

The general manager and the production stage manager have little or nothing to do with the kind and style of show selected. All of these essential contributions will be discussed individually.

The producer, however, must assume all of the responsibilities connected with the production. The show itself is often his own choice, or, in the nonprofessional theater, a decision made by "committee." This selection will be based on the satisfactory answer to three major considerations: Can this show be reasonably well cast with the performers the producer has access to? Will his potential audience find his choice of show appealing? Will the money he has available, or can raise, be adequate for the cost of scenery, costumes, props, advertising, and whatever other special local costs he will encounter? More clearly, will he operate at a profit or a loss?

If the nonprofessional producer manages to get his show on without exceeding his budget, he enjoys a sense of accomplishment because he has given himself a particularly firm status with his superiors. While this is, in itself, an achievement that will generate a sense of faith in his know-how, his other accomplishment is in the enjoyment he has been able to provide his audience. If he operates at a profit, his next undertaking will be looked on as a "reasonable" one.

In a sense, the nonprofessional producer has fewer problems than his professional counterpart, since he is not concerned with long runs, expensive advertising, and the demands describing working hours, number of personnel, and minimum salaries that are prescribed by the unions (for stagehands, actors, designers, musicians, and so on).

It is impossible to generalize about union demands. They vary geographically, according to the size and availability of local membership, the *apparent* wealth of the producing organization, the size of the auditorium, number of performances, ticket prices, and, very often, whether or not there are any professional performers or stars in the production.

Sometimes the actual producing organizations and the performances are situated in a very small town—perhaps a college town. However, a particular town may be only 40 or 50 miles away from a city where unions are active because "road shows" (traveling professional companies) appear from time to time. In this situation, the small nonprofessional production may suddenly come within the jurisdiction of unions.

Each case is different. Among once-active unionized orchestra players, there may have been so little employment in the last decade or so that the musicians will have turned to other jobs. They may not have kept in shape technically, or their "regular" work may occupy hours that would interfere with rehearsals or even performances. These people might not feel prepared to play and will not want to jeopardize their working positions in order to participate perhaps once or twice a year in a theatrical production, so they will not be available to satisfy any union demand for the hiring of professional musicians.

In a school production, "key" professional players, that is, the leaders of a section (first trumpet, first reed, concertmaster, and so on) will sometimes be used in order to enhance the orchestral quality and security. Sometimes "key" personnel are largely teachers within the school.

Most unions are governed by boards. In my own experience, these boards have usually behaved in a reasonable fashion. They listen to the petitioner's problems and try to be as helpful as possible, providing their leniency does not seem to threaten the union itself by establishing a precedent that can be invoked by other organizations not entitled to special treatment.

The producer, with the help of the stage director, must compute the amount of rehearsal time needed to get the show on the stage. Computing the necessary time and scheduling are detailed in Chapter 3, but the nonprofessional producer must familiarize himself with all of the local problems as regards time and money.

The nonprofessional producer may have to "wear two hats"—that of producer and general manager. Many high schools and colleges do not have general managers, possibly because the need for such a position has not occurred to them. Without one, the producer's time and attention, which should be directed to problems other than financial, can become so dispersed that the entire show-in-progress can suffer. In negotiating amateur productions, there must be a realistic budget that is based on a summary of *all* costs: rental of the show itself, purchase of material for scenery, advertising in one or several forms, costume rental or creation, cost of additional lighting equipment (new gelatins, bulbs), and so on. The solution of these problems should be a part of the producer's function *before* the initial budget has been drawn and approved, not after.

The title "producer" may not be employed in all nonprofessional theaters. However, an equivalent position must exist. The first thing anyone needs to learn about theater (musical theater in particular, since it involves participation by so many people) is that it is not, never has been, and never can be a democratic institution. It cannot be run successfully by vote. Productions must be "governed" from a single point of view, and every participant must be willing to adhere to the dictates of one person at the top. This person—with or without a title—is indeed the producer. He has the vision, the know-how to run things, and, if he is frustrated or interfered with, his vision will become confused and the resultant production must suffer.

After all, it *is* the producer's responsibility not only to approve the choice of the show he plans to mount, but to oversee casting; approve the director's and choreographer's work-in-progress; consent to the director's scenic preferences; observe the musical director's progress; and regulate the dozens of other operations that can contribute significantly to his project, the success or failure of which will reflect on him.

The following are the department heads who will work on the show:

stage director

stage manager

scene designer

costume designer

lighting designer

choreographer

musical director

public relations head (whose department includes advertising)

house manager (charges include box office, ushers, auditorium, etc.)

As noted earlier, it is possible, especially in the smaller nonprofessional theater, that some of these positions can be eliminated through consolidation. The scene and costume designs may be created by one person. Lighting may be done by this designer, by the stage director, or by the stage manager. There is no doubt, however, that dividing the chores into separate departments can lighten and hasten the workload, and perhaps it can also broaden the production point of view through the necessity of discussion and collaboration.

Now let us consider each department head separately and define the activity for which each will be responsible. It should be understood that, at times, two or more departments will need to work together cooperatively. However, *all* of them must collaborate if the show is to enjoy maximum success.

Although the producer may decide upon the specific project and engage or assign to the various departments the people he considers the best qualified, once a department head has been designated, that person's responsibilities begin. He must operate with due authority, at the same time working collaboratively with everyone under and alongside him.

The stage director is indeed the artistic head of the project. The reader should be reminded of the fact that, in the creation of a theater piece, in the casting and assembling of its many parts, there can be no democracy! Although the stage director should listen carefully to suggestions from authorized and experienced co-workers, he is the artistic tsar and must be decisive—there can be no deviation between his intention and its realization.

The stage manager, already mentioned, observes carefully everything the director prescribes. He makes notes of all stage directions, supervises rehearsal schedules, insures the presence of personnel and material needed at rehearsals and performances. He is the keeper of discipline and, at performances, runs the show.

The scene designer first formulates his ideas, but without "freezing" them, from reading the script and listening to the music. In this way, the style of the show *as it exists on paper* is at least suggested. He should not become rigid about any ideas until he and his co-artists have discussed the project with the director, who may have a special concept in mind. Once the basic concept is established and understood, the scene de-

7

signer will have to come to grips with the production schedule so as to be able to deliver the scenery—constructed and painted—at precisely the right time.

Often a scene designer will double as costume designer; if, however, these are two distinct positions for a given play, the two designers will need to collaborate in choice of colors and basic style. Again, the costume designer must take into account the amount of time allotted and must insist on taking the measurements of all performers even before rehearsal begins, so that work on making the costumes can proceed.

The lighting designer in our own time is a separate person. Historically, his work was done by the director or the scene designer. (It is not unheard of in the nonprofessional theater to consolidate this position with another.) If, however, he *is* a third designer, he will need to work closely with scene and costume designers as well as the stage director and choreographer in order to know where his equipment, physically, and his talents, aesthetically, can be must useful and effective.

The choreographer in the nonprofessional theater will not have to be a partner in the creation of dance music, nor will he be required to search out places for dancing in the show. In the production of a revival, the placement of dances and the music will already be defined in the score. He will, however, need to consider carefully the capabilities of the dancers available to him. He will also need to understand specifically how his personal style of dance and choreography can be best related to the needs of the show—and of course he is a full partner in the casting process.

The musical director, too, must have a strong say in casting so that he provides himself with the necessary singers in the vocal ensemble and is certain that the principals are able to negotiate the songs *as written.* As with the other members of the staff, his rehearsals and performance duties are spelled out in a subsequent chapter. In terms of responsibility, the choreographer and the stage director will have completed their work when the curtain rises; the stage manager and the musical director continue to operate throughout all performances.

The public relations chief should have close personal contacts with the editors of local newspapers and radio and TV stations—the "Amusements" editor, the society editor, and the one assigned to special events and "features." This public relations head must know how to write "copy" (stories) and releases that, if accepted, are not in need of rewriting or extensive editing. He must have a feeling for what a particular editor of a specific paper or station would be most apt to report. He should know how to take advantage of seasonal holidays (Easter, Christmas); the weather (snow, spring, and so on); and local celebrations. He should know everything that it is possible for him to find out about the particular show he is promoting—when it was first produced, who were its stars, writers, composers, and all kinds of "human interest" tales connected with it—that could be of interest to his potential audience. He must know *when* to start his publicity campaign, when to accelerate it, and how to vary his releases so that the public does not become inundated with information it could conceive as "repetitious." He must be aware that *secrecy* does not sell tickets.

Each of these department heads has his own responsibility for accomplishing the most effective results with the show at hand. Each one is responsible for completing his part of the work within the time allotted and agreed upon. He must be familiar with deadlines. He must know how to collaborate, to be helpful to his peers, and finally how to integrate his own contribution into the work as a whole and not make it so "unusual" that it seems to be attempting to outdo everything else.

It is the department heads' separate accomplishments as well as their "participation" that will help to make the most out of the production as a whole.

The collaborative activity needs to be set in motion by the producer and watched over by him—he must never forget that the realization of the show is his responsibility, the successful outcome of the production his job.

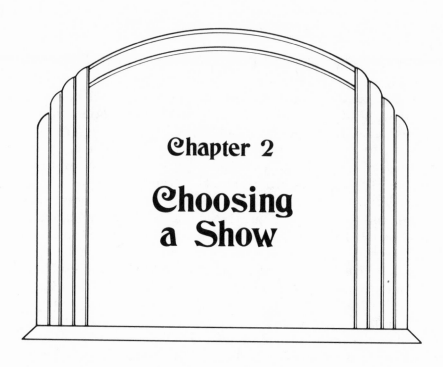

Chapter 2

Choosing a Show

THE CHOICE OF one of several already-produced musical shows for re-production depends on many more factors than liking a particular show, or enjoying songs from its score. These factors in general are:

cost of production

size of cast

degree of difficulty in casting

average age of audience to be attracted

general audience appeal

the time in which the action takes place

The cost of production is extremely flexible. The scenery—regardless of the list of sets called for in the libretto—can be "abstracted" so that even the use of a unit set* is possible. The cost of costumes will vary with the size of the cast and the historical period in which the action takes place. The size of the orchestra in a nonprofessional theater may not affect the production cost since such orchestras are, as a rule, nonunion, and most often the players are students and/or instructors.

The size of the cast does not have to be determined by the number of characters listed in the show. For example, the original production of *Li'l Abner* lists 35 characters, yet eight actors played two parts each and two performers played three. This reduced the cast personnel to 23—not 35—people. If it were desirable in a revival of *Li'l Abner* to employ *more* performers in the cast, there could be 35 (no doubling of parts), and there is even the possibility of adding a few others as "merry villagers."

In the use of orchestra musicians—provided an orchestra is employed—string parts can be added. For example, in the same show *(Li'l Abner)* the Tams-Witmark catalogue (to be spoken of later) is most thorough. It lists strings as "violin AC and violin BD, viola, cello, bass." Translated, this means that there are four *different* violin parts, and only a single part each for viola, cello, and bass. However, there can be as many AC and BD players as desired so long as these additional music scores are procured. There can be four, five, six, or more violas and cellos, and two or three basses. The most decisive factor to be considered carefully in expanding the orchestra is the size of the orchestra pit, which might or might not allow for many extra players. Orchestra volume can be controlled by the musical director. On Broadway, the average musical employs 25 players according to union minimum requirement. Fitting 25 men with their chairs, music stands, and instruments into the average Broadway pit is very much like putting the pieces of a jigsaw puzzle together.

Still using *Li'l Abner* for this discussion, there are five reeds listed. Each calls for four instruments except reed five, which uses only three. Tams-Witmark has, however, reduced these

---

*One single structure that, with changes of lighting (now more important than ever), can suggest in more or less abstract fashion different places and times.

parts (if reduction is desired) to *two* instruments for each of the five reed players: reed one, for example, has been alternately scored for clarinet and alto sax, whereas originally that player used clarinet, alto sax, flute, and piccolo. It is possible that a single local musician does not play both clarinet and alto sax, in which case two players can play from the single part—one playing *only* clarinet, the other, *only* alto sax.

In today's music world, "combos" are in vogue. Sometimes this is due to economics, but more often it is because people have become accustomed to the electronic sound and the small group of players.

Rental agencies generally refuse to break up sets of orchestra parts. This means that the Rodgers and Hammerstein Library (the rental agency), for example, has packaged many complete sets of the orchestra parts of *Oklahoma!* They would not be willing to break up a set in order to extract the parts for double bass, trumpet, drums, and first reed. This need not deter the nonprofessional group that would like to employ a small combo. The bass part can be played from the vocal score that the pianist will be using. A drummer can "create" a rhythm pattern for each number provided the musical director *tastefully* designates precisely when he is *not* to play, and what *precise* instrument in the percussionist's "kitchen" he is to use—number by number.

Using a trumpet or a reed instrument is more complicated, since the parts would need to be written out, "created" from the same vocal score. However, use of piano, double bass, and drums poses no insurmountable problems. Certainly the sound of a combo is preferable to that of a poor band. The audience has come to see and hear a musical show. An out-of-tune band that overpowers the singers on the stage interferes with the joy of experiencing the show as a whole, and the band should be eliminated in favor of the more modest, more flexible, and quieter combo.

Orchestra, choral, and spoken parts (called "sides") can be rented as far in advance of performance as the directors deem necessary. The singers can start to learn their parts three months in advance if the rehearsal schedule will of necessity be interrupted by examinations, holidays, and other local interferences.

The orchestra may have not only the same regular interruptions, but additional events to rehearse and perform for:
concerts, broadcasts, ballgames, and so on. In many schools
the instrumental players form several different units. There
may be a large concert band, a smaller marching band, a
dance band, and an orchestra. A number of players will be
members of two or more of these units, and each unit has a
schedule of rehearsals and performances.

If an orchestra is to be employed for a musical show, the
exact instrumentation required should be given to the head of
the appropriate department, and a realistic discussion take
place as to possible rehearsal and performance schedules as
planned by the musical theater "producer." If matters can be
firmly agreed upon, the production can be immeasurably en-
hanced, but no detail of schedule should be left to chance. If
other activities interfere with learning the show, separate parts
may be taken home and worked on individually whenever a
free hour presents itself, provided the producer has secured
the parts early enough to allow for such helpful extra practice
time.

Published librettos and even rental-agency catalogues can
be frightening as regards scenery. For example, the scenic list
for *Man of La Mancha* numbers 23 sets, yet, in the original
New York production, there was only one basic or unit set
with inserts and a stunning long staircase that was lowered
from high above onto the stage at a 45-degree angle. While
the latter was one of the most effective aspects of the production, it is conceivable that, if such a mechanical contrivance
were not possible or feasible, the show could be done without
it.

Company, in the published libretto, is divided into two acts,
with six scenes in the first act and five in the second. Yet there
is a basic

> multi-leveled steel structure indicating various high-rise Manhat-
> tan apartments. Two elevators and stairs link the different levels.
> There are five empty living areas on the various levels of the
> raised structure. Each of the areas is to denote the apartment of
> one couple, and it is that same area to which the couple will al-
> ways return at various points during the action. When cleared,
> the stage level belongs to Robert . . . most of the larger scenes

13

are played in this stage-level area, with sections containing furniture moved on . . . rear and frontal projections are used to indicate different skylines and city sights.*

One moveable structure and the judicious use of lights spelled out the original production, which was clear as to locale and always interesting. While the central structure was the feature of Boris Aronson's production, it is conceivable that, with proper lighting, the show could be reproduced on a bare stage. But then, so could almost any show.

Similarly, the nonmusical play *Equus* by Peter Shaffer describes the single set as "a square of wood set on a circle of wood. The square resembles a railed boxing ring. . . ." The audience's imagination is greatly aided by lighting changes, and the text of the play "allows" the audience to envision a psychiatrist's office, a middle-class house interior, a beach, a stable, a meadow, a shop, a movie house, and a number of other largely transitional places.

In discussing a show for revival, let us consider for a moment *The Student Prince* as the hypothetical choice. Several major factors should enter into the selection of this lovely (if dated) operetta for production. After all, the choice, although arrived at on a unilateral basis—the producer's decision representative of his personal taste—should not be conclusive unless it considers seriously, for example, three factors concerning audience: the production cost, the average age of ticket-buyers, and their taste.

The most obvious first consideration, it occurs to me, is how often *The Student Prince* has been presented in the theater contemplating a new production, and over how long a period of time. The Dallas Summer Operetta's repertoire gives its own answers and provides a look at the "death of kings":

The Student Prince, 1941, 1945, 1947, and 1952

Rose Marie, 1941, 1943, 1946, 1949, and 1957

The Desert Song, 1941, 1944, 1947, 1950, and 1968

*From the published libretto of *Company.*

The infiltration of new shows as they became available is most interesting, although the following list of Dallas productions is not exhaustive, and Dallas is not very different in most respects from St. Louis, Kansas City, and a number of other large summer musical theaters:

Pal Joey, 1949

Where's Charley?, 1951

I Married an Angel, 1951

Carousel, 1952, 1955, and 1962

South Pacific, 1955, 1957, 1962, and 1967

Oklahoma!, 1958, 1966, and 1973

West Side Story, 1960 and 1966

Note that, by 1949, a gradual invasion of new shows became evident and, with the revival of *The Desert Song* in 1968, the most popular of all American operettas became extinct, at least in Dallas, Texas. Note also that no show appeared in the repertoire in two consecutive seasons and that five revivals of a work occurred in only two cases: *Rose Marie,* five times in 16 years, and *The Desert Song,* five times in 27 years.

With the gradual inclusion of new Broadway shows as they became available, the operettas of the 1920s were phased out, just as, prior to the American operettas, the Gilbert & Sullivan repertoire had ruled the rosters nearly everywhere and was then dropped altogether.*

Before going ahead to consider other factors affecting repertoire selection, it is interesting to note that the practice of elimination of the old and *steady* inclusion of the new is less discernible if one examines the Metropolitan Opera schedule. Among many other "favorites," *Aida* made its Met debut (in German) in 1886 (it was then 5 years old), *Carmen* (in Italian) in 1884 (9 years old), *Lucia Di Lammermoor* in 1883 (48 years old), and *Madama Butterfly* in 1907 (3 years old). There has sel-

*Nothing very good is ever very dead. In 1980–81 *The Pirates of Penzance* became a big hit in New York and in Los Angeles, and will probably have an entire new existence in subsequent productions.

dom been a season—in some cases in more than a century—
without these and other staples. On the other hand, almost
annually there have been new American operas and works by
contemporary Europeans that have seldom been repeated in
another season. Among those have been Hadley's *Cleopatra's
Night*, Damrosch's *Cyrano*, Gruenberg's *The Emperor Jones*,
Menotti's *The Island God*, Hanson's *Merry Mount*, and Deems
Taylor's *Peter Ibbetson*. The Barber-Menotti *Vanessa*, which has
been scheduled during seasons other than its premiere, has
been repeated occasionally, and *Wozzeck* is heard in many seasons, but these works are the exceptions.

One can only guess at differences between opera and musical theater customers, but it is obvious that the same principles do not apply.

The show most in demand for revival today is *Oklahoma!*,
written in 1943. However, the list of other shows popular with
nonprofessional theater audiences is nearly endless. This pop-
ularity is due, first, to the appeal of the shows themselves. But
this appeal has been intensified by recordings, television, radio, and films, which have unwittingly joined hands to echo
the best of Broadway's past over and over to audiences everywhere in the world.

*   *   *

There are many considerations with which we should come
to grips in deciding upon a revival:

Can this show be cast satisfactorily?

What is the average age of the audience?

Can the scenic requirements be provided?

Will the accompaniment consist of one piano, two pianos,
an orchestra, or a combo?

Can the cast and ensemble be reduced in size (probably a
Broadway question) or can it be expanded (desirable in
many schools)?

What available rehearsal time can be counted on (especially
for schools); therefore, how many weeks or months

ahead of performance will be needed for preparation, and then when will the show open and how many performances are planned?

Are there available personnel to form a competent staff?

What is the budgetary requirement of this show, and is that money definitely available?

Is the libretto workable today as it exists, or will it need small or extensive rewriting or editing?

Is necessary rehearsal space available for the period of rehearsals, and is the theater likewise free of other commitments for the show's final preparation, technical and dress rehearsals, and the scheduled performances?

Will the selection of this particular show engender enthusiasm in the performers, the directorate, and the local audiences?

All of these questions need careful consideration in advance of any firm decisions. Let us examine some of them separately.

"Can this show be cast satisfactorily?"

Let us contemplate several hypothetical problems that can arise. I think this casting question must begin with the most difficult problem.

If a group were desirous of presenting Victor Herbert's *Naughty Marietta,* they should note that the most demanding song—"The Italian Street Song"—is sung by a lyric-coloratura heroine. She must have the technique to sing florid passages clearly and with ease. Her range is from low D to high C, with many high A's and B-flats. If these vocal difficulties provide no stumbling block, is the female who is able to cope satisfactorily with them also young, attractive, and possessed of a good figure? She is the young heroine (Marietta) and must sing, look, and act the role.

Let us take another and different kind of show for an ex-

17

ample. Suppose we wish to present *Gypsy* by Jule Styne, Stephen Sondheim, and Arthur Laurents. By far the most difficult role is that of Rose, the mother, played originally by Ethel Merman. The problems will come into focus more quickly if we think of the original casting—not because we wish to imitate it but because we can see at once the style and quality expected of the performer. Rose should appear to be middle-aged: she is the mother of two (eventually) grown girls. She must be able to act with tough deliberation and with great warmth. Merman's vocal delivery was in "chest." She belted much of "Rose's Turn," the most demanding of all of her songs. Its tessitura is low and often hangs around low A-flat. It's highest note is the B in the middle of the treble clef.

Questions of vocal type and range, physical appearance, and acting capacity are not the only primary requirements for casting of a difficult role. Frequently an exceptional characteristic will be demanded as well.

In *West Side Story*, Tony and Maria, the two leads, must move (dance) as well as they sing and act.

In *My Fair Lady*, Eliza Doolittle must sing and act, but she must also necessarily be able to simulate a *convincing* Cockney accent, which will, in the unfolding of the show, be transformed into upper-class British speech. Without this ability, the entire point of the show will be meaningless.

In *The Most Happy Fella*, the hero, Tony, must look middle-aged, balding, and somewhat overweight, must sing in a "legitimate" high baritone voice—almost operatic in style and production—and must be able to speak English with a pronounced Italian accent. In stating these requirements, I am not resorting to memory of the original production but to basic physical demands of the libretto that must be fulfilled. If Tony is *not* middle-aged, balding, and overweight, the chief problems that create the conflict in the show will not present themselves, and then there will be no show! Tony is insecure because Rosabella (his "mail-order bride") is young and pretty. This intensifies Tony's feeling of unworthiness, as a result of which he sends Rosabella a photograph of his handsome ranch foreman (saying that it is a picture of himself), and this produces shock when she first encounters him as "an *old* man,

18

an *old* man." In fact, the show receives its thrust from Tony's insecurity, which would not exist if he were young, had a trim figure and a full head of hair, and spoke English without an accent.

In every case, the requirements for casting a character in a show—especially a leading one—are implicit in the libretto itself.

"What is the average age of the audience?"

Audiences for a college campus production will come mainly from the student body, although there will also be some instructors with their families, relatives of cast members, and local townspeople. As far as appeal to the youthful element is concerned, there can be several choices that go beyond the obvious selections.

One decision would be the choice of a show involving predominately young characters, although I am advised this is not necessarily a factor. Under the school aegis, with its abundance of eager participants, casting young characters with young performers if the easiest way. Among the shows that present this opportunity are:

Bye Bye Birdie	*West Side Story*
Best Foot Forward	*Grease*
Hair	*Babes in Arms*
A Chorus Line	

While selection of a show involving young people, for young audiences, and with a cast of young people is in every way obvious, there is another consideration. The "musical comedy" which evolved in its heyday to "musical theater" produced very successful shows that engendered considerable audience emotion. In my own experience, shows that truly involve audience emotions appeal to people of *all* ages everywhere. Viewed from this perspective, the choice-spec-

19

trum becomes greatly enlarged. The shows in the following list (among many others) seem to affect people of all ages:

Carousel	*The Sound of Music*
Fiddler on the Roof	*Oklahoma!*
Annie	*Guys and Dolls*
Hello, Dolly!	*Fanny*
Cabaret	

Today most people in the 16 to 23 age group have been inculcated with recordings of various styles of rock music. Much rock is heard in contemporary films and on television. It would *seem*, therefore, that only rock shows would appeal to young audiences. This is not the case. Rock performers attract large audiences, and rock recordings sell far more than any others, but the rock musical theater seems to have passed through its heyday in the sixties. It has all but disappeared completely as a theater form. Reasons can be surmised, but they contribute nothing to this discussion.

If the Broadway experience is of any value, *The King and I* revival of 1977 was enormously successful. *Fiddler on the Roof* ran 167 performances in 1976 and had another successful Broadway revival in 1981. *Guys and Dolls* and *My Fair Lady* did moderately well when brought back to Broadway, but the revival of *Hair* was a disaster.

My only hint of an explanation of the rock craze versus what I call "classical" American musical theater style is that the young people consider the former in a nontheater perspective and the latter as musical theater. They seem to relish not only observing the "classics" as audience but also participating in them whenever they have the opportunity.

And so it would seem that young audiences do not eschew the musical shows that succeeded so well in the 1940–1965 period, and their seniors seem to continue to regard these same shows as "old friends."

One *possible* clue to the ambivalence in the taste of young theatergoers may be found in the existence of the romantic plot in the more traditional shows, plus the comedy contrast that complements the basic romantic conflict—these do not exist in rock shows. No attempt is made to include them. The rock "concert," which attracts huge audiences for one or two performances in enormous auditoriums, lures its adherents through rhythmic insistence, deafening amplification, and a youthful empathy that includes sexual insinuation and kinetic vivacity: propulsion as opposed to expression and feeling generated in all of the other senses.

If the age of the audience for a prospective musical revival is generally adult, some other important considerations present themselves: what is their regional background, what is the general education level, and do they represent staunchly a single religious affiliation?

The presenters of the show must think seriously about, let us say, a southwest rural audience: would it prefer *Oklahoma!* or something in a more sophisticated idiom that might provide a greater opportunity to experience a lifestyle with which they were less familiar? This question can only be answered properly in each specific circumstance. Many people derive great pleasure from seeing shows that celebrate their prototypes. Others prefer something more "exotic." In the hypothesis suggested above, if the latter feeling were strongest, that kind of audience might enjoy:

Guys and Dolls	*Fiddler on the Roof*
Cabaret	*A Little Night Music*
Hello, Dolly!	*Company*
Mame	

"Can the scenic requirements be provided?"

The answer to this is an almost unqualified "yes." Shows such as *Annie Get Your Gun, South Pacific,* and *The Pajama Game,* to name only a few, were created in an era when multi-scene musicals employed the device of the "traveler curtain"*—

*To be discussed in chap. 7.

the kind that comes together from each side of the stage, meeting at stage-center to allow what are called "cross-overs." These consisted usually of song reprises, parades, "walking" dialogue scenes, or almost anything that might retain the audience's attention while the scenery behind the curtains was being shifted.

Today, there are more shows done with unit sets. A slider, or wagon (a small bit of sliding flooring mounted on rollers), can be wheeled on stage from either side. On the top of the slider there can be one or two pieces of furniture, sometimes backed by a folding screen or a hanging picture that would suggest a particular kind of room or locale and its quality—rich, poor, middle-class, and so on. Sometimes there has been sketchy scenery, small bits that could be pulled on- or off-stage in view of the audience.

Fairly recent musicals representative of this style are:

Company	*Shenandoah*
A Little Night Music	*The Robber Bridegroom*
I Love My Wife	*Sweeney Todd*
Pippin	

For a long time now there have been plays (nonmusicals) with minimal or no scenery. These have included:

Equus	*The Basic Training of Pavlo Hummel*
The Royal Hunt of the Sun	
Our Town (and other short plays by Thornton Wilder)	*Waiting for Godot*

"What is the Budgetary Requirement of This Show and is That Money Definitely Available?"

The financing of a production, whether on Broadway or in the nonprofessional theater, must be carefully assured. This matter of finance is, of course, the Broadway producer's first concern. In the nonprofessional theater, there are no unions to deal with, no minimum salaries, no legal stipulations as to allowable working hours, and (most often) no rent. Scenery and costumes are made by local personnel, props are usually borrowed, and orchestrations (when used) are rented along with the leasing of rights to perform the show. The lighting equipment that has already been installed as an integral part of the theater can be refocused, rehung, and employed to bring to life whatever is to take place on the stage. Switchboards are already present, waiting to be activated.

And so the costs to producers in nonprofessional theaters have little to do with personnel in creating or performing the production. But nonprofessional producers *must* pay for materials that will be converted into scenery and costumes, and fees for leasing the show for performance.

Since most personnel are unpaid,* it follows that those who build and paint, sing and dance, play instruments, and those who direct do so because they want to participate and are willing to give all of the time they can cut loose from school schedules or from earning a living. In a sense, this attitude and the effort that it requires represent the purest kind of theater. The results will be the best that the collection of personnel is capable of producing, and will have been activated solely by the desire to participate in the creation of a special world.

The producer, who must maintain control, who must choose the personnel and see that they function well and adhere to their schedule—however slack it may seem to professional theater workers—must reconcile his dreams with these responsibilities.

*　　*　　*

The four principal rental agencies from which you can obtain musical shows are:

*In some community theaters today, some directors, technical directors, and business managers are salaried.

Tams-Witmark Music Library, Inc. (TW)
560 Lexington Avenue
New York, N.Y. 10022
(212) MU 8-2525
(Toll free—800-221-7196; in N.Y. State: 800-522-2181)

Music Theatre International (MTI)
119 West 57th Street
New York, N.Y. 10019
(212) 975-6841

Samuel French, Inc. (SF)
25 West 45th Street
New York, N.Y. 10036
(212) JU 2-4700

The Rodgers and Hammerstein Library (R&H)
598 Madison Avenue
New York, N.Y. 10022
(212) 486-0643

For a small fee plus postage, these agencies will send perusal copies of the scripts and scores of any of the shows in their catalogues. Broadway orchestrations are available for rental, and there are also some arrangements for band, combos, and sometimes two-piano versions. (Deposits are sometimes required for this musical material.)

In the Introduction to the Tams-Witmark catalogue, the general arrangements are spelled out:

> Our royalties are based on your admission prices, capacity of your auditorium, dates and number of performances and whether you require an orchestration. The material consists of prompt books, conductor scores, dialogue parts, chorus parts, vocal parts, orchestrations and often stage directions.

The properties offered by TW, MTI, SF, and R&H consist of musical comedies, operettas, revues, shows for children, and a few operas. See Appendix A for an alphabetical listing of the shows for which the most information is available. The entries include the agency, orchestration, cast requirements, number of sets, a brief digest of the plot, a list of the best-known songs, and the record album when one (or more) exists.

Appendix B comprises lists of shows that are also named in each of the four catalogues, but for which the general information readily available is so scarce that any producer potentially interested in presenting any of these shows should write a letter requesting fuller information from the license-contractor. There are countless musical shows that have had first-class productions but have, for one reason or another, never been offered for rental. Usually this is because the show was unsuccessful, and scripts and music for most of these shows would be difficult if not impossible to locate and obtain.

In addition, a few newer musical shows become available each year after the Broadway closing, or the completed National Tour, or the release of the film. Producers should place their own names on the mailing lists of each of the licensing companies.

Chapter 3

Production
Stage Manager
and Schedules

MANY COLLABORATORS in musical theater are unknown to the general public. Few of the millions of theatergoers can tell you anything about the show they have just seen except perhaps the star and the show's title—never the names of the composer; lyricist; librettist; scene, costume, and lighting designers; director; choreographer; producer; conductor; and many, many others who shared the work of putting together the evening's entertainment. Yet it is this army of unidentified people that made "Miss Thelma" look, act, sing, and dance so well.

Frequently a well-known performer will be credited with things for which he or she was not responsible. A man turns to his companion during a performance and remarks, "That woman is the funniest creature I've ever seen," when what he means is, "That writer is. . . ."

No one is more important in his special way than the production stage manager, but, outside of the theatrical profession, he is faceless and unappreciated. In the hierarchy of musical theater, *he* is the man who actually runs the show!

Let us begin with his duties and responsibilities. Throughout auditions and rehearsals, he is always at the side of the stage director. He manages to keep peace and order among the hordes of people who attend the auditions; collects the names, addresses, and telephone numbers of auditionees; usually announces them by name or number to those who are watching or listening; and often makes his own notes concerning certain people. (During one particular audition for singers at which I was present, the stage manager rushed into the theater to say that the next girl was an impossible troublemaker. Yet she was beautiful and sang well, and was subsequently selected over the stage manager's warning. A few days after rehearsals began, she had caused so many disturbances among other members of the cast that she was fired.)

The stage manager runs not one but perhaps a dozen auditions: performers reading and singing for leading roles; ensemble singers, male and female; ensemble dancers, male and female. Between and among these many hours, he keeps meticulous records of those who appeared, including notes given him concerning their desirability, or even remarks overheard from the various directors. He usually anticipates important selections and knows factual matter about those auditioning that will make specific selection easier, more difficult, or impossible. He seems never to lose an agent's name or a performer's name, address, and telephone number. He supplements all of this with his own knowledge—gained from others, or personally experienced—regarding the faults and virtues of certain performers whose qualifications are in question.

After final auditions are held and the various directors have agreed on a cast, the stage manager makes a careful list of those chosen so as to be able to notify them individually (or on Broadway, through their agents) of their acceptance, asking them to come to the producer's office within the next day or two to sign contracts.

The stage manager is also prepared with an all-important list of "second choices" or alternates so that in the (not unusual) event that some people have decided not to do the show, find the salary unacceptable, have an offer of a better part in another show, have to go home to Kansas to take care of family problems—and dozens of other well-known reasons—he can remind the directorate of who else was well liked and arrange for those performers to come to the office* either for further auditions or to sign contracts.

Prior to the start of rehearsals for the entire company, which will take place a week or two after final auditions, the stage manager has a long list of tasks.

Scripts in sufficient quantities must have come from the mimeographer. (In the nonprofessional theater, scripts and music should have been received at least two weeks ahead of the first rehearsals so that there is no doubt whatsoever about their being on hand when they are needed.)

The production stage manager will have checked with the music department to know if it lacks any material, chairs, or whatever might be essential. Is there to be one pianist each for the musical director, stage director, and choreographer? He will "snoop" at the scene and costume designers' studios to see that there are no snags, and with the building and painting studios to be certain they have received designs and have begun to execute them. Finally, he will telephone all members of the cast to insure their being present *and on time* on (for example) next Wednesday morning at 10 A.M. at the Such and Such Studios.

All of that attended to, and with one or two assistants engaged, he will scale down the studio floor space to correspond to the floor plan of each set. He will then mark the floor with colored Scotch tape: scene 1 outlined accurately (proportionately) in red; scene 2 in green; scene 3, yellow; and so on. In this way the actors can note their relationship to the set and the director can anticipate many of his subsequent problems. Not only are the set outlines described, but steps, doorways, and so on, are also outlined—whatever can help the per-

---

*It is *not* advisable to hold ensemble auditions more than four weeks prior to the start of rehearsals lest auditionees get better opportunities that start them to work at once!

former to become acquainted with limits of the real set that will be encountered only a few days prior to the first performance.

At rehearsals, the production stage manager calls the company to order, makes any announcements he may have, including schedules, and (on Broadway) reads the Equity rules. Seldom straying far from the stage director's side throughout rehearsals, he continually makes notes in his script (this becomes known as the "prompt copy"). Usually he places blank pages between the mimeographed script pages and transcribes onto the blank pages every move the director decrees, marks carefully every word that is either cut or added, and notates any direction that is given. His "prompt copy" becomes the Bible of the show.

In recent years, musical shows have begun rehearsing in studios instead of theaters because all of the latter have been occupied. When rehearsals took place in theaters, the stage director nearly always exercised his prerogative to rehearse on the stage, leaving the choreographer to take his dancers downstairs to the lounge or the ladies' room. Individual song and choral rehearsals took place *only* when the stage was not occupied, with the singers seated in the first two rows of the auditorium and a pianist in the pit. Lighting was seldom adequate; the director had to content himself with a "work light"—a naked bulb attached to an iron stand, usually placed in the middle of the stage, but moveable.

While there were sometimes objections to this "split" procedure, the practice turned into a blessing, and the same method has been adapted to studio use.

In studios there are ideally—under one roof—two large rooms, as nearly as possible the size of the actual stage. One of these is used by the stage director, the other by the choreographer. There is usually a fair-sized room for ensemble singing and one or two very tiny "practice rooms" just large enough to hold an upright piano and a couple of chairs.

It is well for those planning to produce musical shows in regional theater or schools to realize that availability of the stage is perhaps a luxury and surely not a necessity. What is much more beneficial is being able to rehearse in a single building that contains at least two spacious rooms (a gymnasium, cafeteria, study hall, etc.) and studios containing pianos.

This arrangement allows many different rehearsals to take place simultaneously, and, if one of the directors needs to borrow for a short time one or two people engaged in another rehearsal, the individuals can be reached at once, take part in the second rehearsal, and returned to their original commitment as soon as possible.

Every rehearsal room should have a piano. There are generally two pianists. (For the first production of an original score—usually on Broadway—there is a third pianist called the dance arranger.) One of these two pianists will be watchful of anyone who is not now being used, take that performer into a practice room, and hammer out the notes of a song he must learn.

In nonprofessional theaters, the availability of three pianists is unrealistic. In that case, the stage director—important as he is to the project as a whole—should have a pianist at his disposal *only* when he is putting together several scenes that have already been blocked and for which the songs have already been rehearsed and memorized. If the musical director is a pianist, he can play his own chorus rehearsals and also accompany principals while coaching them in the songs. Today, dancers often rehearse to taped music in many theaters.

In school and regional circumstances, it is most necessary that the theater in which the performances will take place be firmly committed to the dates of performances, that performances be preceded by technical and dress rehearsals, and that these be consecutive! I can think of nothing more nightmarish than scheduling three rehearsals (one technical and two dress) on three consecutive nights, then finding the theater scheduled for some other activity the night before opening!

As to rehearsals, in the professional theater Actors' Equity allows its members to work seven out of ten hours daily, with one day in seven off. (On Broadway, principals in a musical can rehearse for up to seven weeks; chorus can rehearse for eight weeks.) The stage director, choreographer, musical director, and production stage manager together work out daily and weekly schedules in such a way as to allow them the most rehearsal time. This means probably that they themselves will have *no* time off, generally because principals are given one free day and the members of the ensembles a different one. Then, too, when it can be arranged, some cast members will be called at 10 A.M. Everyone will break for lunch from 1 to 2:30 P.M. At 2:30 *everyone* will be called. The ones required to come at 10 A.M. will be finished at 6:30 P.M. At that time, there will be a supper break until 8. At *that* time, those who were not called until 2:30 P.M. will return and work until 11.

Among the vastly different nonprofessional groups, the foregoing schedule would not work *except* in principle. Of course, there will be no union requirement restricting maximum number of rehearsal weeks; three months of rehearsal is not unusual on the nonprofessional level. If the group exists within a school, class hours must be considered before anything else. If it is a community theater, participants have jobs or housework. In that case, evenings and weekends will yield the necessary time.

However, it is the *amount* of available time in all cases that must be considered. *Ideally,* in the school situation, rehearsals might be from 4 to 6 P.M. and 7:30 to 10:30 P.M.—five hours daily—with possibly ten hours on Saturday and Sunday. These would total 45 weekly hours—ideal, but rarely possible in most college theaters. Therefore, an effective compromise must be reached. (Who said it was easy? But do you really want to put on a good show? Actually, on Broadway only 42 weekly rehearsal hours per person are allowed.)

In the *ideal* community theater condition, rehearsals might be held on five weekday evenings from, for example, 6 to 11 P.M. and two weekend days of ten hours each, also totaling 45 hours weekly. Again, this would be an extremely difficult schedule for working people to meet, and so the best possible arrangements must be made.

It is my recommendation that, in the beginning, *all* rehearsals be given over to learning songs and dances. After one week devoted exclusively to these, allow only two or three hours daily, then one or two later on (the fourth week and after, if needed), to keep things in trim. Beginning the second week, the stage director would have perhaps three hours nightly and six or seven hours on Saturday and Sunday. The weekend hours might be divided as follows: 10 A.M. to 3 P.M., and 5 P.M. to 10 P.M.

During a period of about four weeks, the entire show should be learned. The stage director will want as many people daily and for as much time as possible. Since both the choreographer and musical director will often want the same people at the same time, there may be a daily argument about what each one *must* have and for how long. And each one has right on his side. The stage manager is the arbiter.

On Broadway, it is desirable that a rough run-through of Act I be ready about the end of the second week. At that time, every member of the staff will try to get a fair idea of how well the show is shaping up, what needs cutting, rewriting, and so on. Each creative person will try to be as self-protective as possible, and it often happens that nobody will want to make big cuts until after a first public performance.

By the end of the third week, Act II will be seen, and, within a day or two, a first run-through of the entire show will take place. Stage, musical, and dance adjustments—usually minor ones—will be made. As each run-through will consume about four hours, only three hours will be available daily for keeping the dances, music, and book in shape.

While the above applies to Broadway, where all personnel must be available daily and for seven hours out of ten, I have included it here to give an idea of what professional rehearsing is like.

In one sense, rehearsing in any kind of nonprofessional situation is easier, since large amounts of time are wasted in rehearsals of new, developing shows. Scenes that have been learned and blocked are rewritten, cut out altogether, or replaced with new scenes. Songs are deleted and replaced. Choruses are likewise replaced, or choral arrangments redone. Dances are created and dance music is composed at the same time. Almost universally, the dances are found to be too long and are reduced in length or, after arduous rehearsing, are found not to work in the context of the show and are eliminated altogether. Opening numbers—the most difficult to pin down—are discarded and replaced. Each creative mishap requires everyone's time and hard work—singers, actors, dancers—in learning an entirely new number or scene.

None of this applies to the nonprofessional theater, since there is little if any rewriting, no song or lyric changes, no new choral arrangements, no new dance music, no new opening number. The people who labor in nonprofessional theater are thus in an advantageous position as regards time. The many hours wasted in putting on a new show will not be wasted in doing one that has already been "shaken down."

However, since rehearsals in the nonprofessional theater will be sporadic, perhaps not daily, not for long consecutive periods of time, and possibly spread out over a longer period of time than was spent originally, the performers—especially ensemble singers and dancers—will most naturally be apt to forget at least part of what they have learned, and time will be required for refreshing their memories and keeping ensemble singing and dancing together.

It is my suggestion that all department heads operating under nonprofessional conditions, taking into account the inevitable interruptions, make out careful schedules beginning (as it is done *also* on Broadway) backward from the end! In other words, the first performance is scheduled for (let us hypothesize) May 30. Then dress and technical rehearsals may occur May 27, 28, and 29. In order for the company to be prepared for these, the number of rehearsal hours should be computed on a (this is guessing) 150-hour availability. (I am deducting 50 hours from the Broadway schedule in lieu of creative changes that will not be necessary here.) The date for *beginning* rehearsals would be not later than April 1, and this date should be preceded by at least two weeks for auditions. Prior to *that* time—March 15 on this schedule—the department heads would need several weeks of discussion, the choreographer would need to begin creating his dances, the scene designer would have begun his layouts with those who will build and paint the scenery, and, not least, the rental agency that controls performance rights would have been contacted several months earlier to insure availability of all rehearsal material.

If the clothes are to be rented, order forms will need to

have been obtained from the costume rental house so that, as soon as the show has been cast, measurements can be taken for every member of the cast and then dispatched to the costume company more than six weeks prior to the first dress rehearsal. In this way, after the clothes arrive they can be tried on and altered, if necessary, by competent local seamstresses. If the measurements have been accurate at the outset, few alterations should be necessary.

On the other hand, if the clothes are to be made locally, the same long lead time is suggested. As soon as the casting is completed, the designers and/or seamstresses will need to take individual measurements. (The designs will have been created and approved ahead of rehearsals.) Some time will have to be given over to fittings, since alterations—even minor ones—will require time to execute.

It is also advisable to divide the total amount of rehearsal time into halves, with the expectation of being able to see Act I at about the halfway mark, then Act II at least five rehearsals before the scheduled technical one. This will allow at least four periods of run-throughs of the entire show prior to the performers' having to become additionally confused with costumes, orchestra, lights, and scenery.

*   *   *

The stage manager will need time away from rehearsals to observe the hanging of lights and scenery so that he will be in a position to order their proper operation during performances. He sees these actually working, learns whether a drop falls, a set comes from stage right on rollers, or a turntable revolves. He needs to see these manipulations so that he can help to clear the scenic working space of performers who might impede the swift change or get in the way and be injured.

During this period, the lighting designer will set cues for the lights. In a musical show there may be 200 cues, and each will involve a number of different lamps in different places so that, working together, they create a single desired effect. Each cue will not only be set, but the proper intensity of each light will be marked. Sometimes an entire effect will go on to a slow count of ten, or twenty, or off in the same way.

The cues are "attached" to various things happening within the show: sometimes to a word, an entrance, an exit, or a bar of music. The production stage manager will note every one of them, giving each a number, because, in performance, he must give the electricians who operate the switches and dimmers a "warning" for each cue and then a "go." These are spoken over a small intercom system (if the theater is so equipped) and are referred to by number.

The production stage manager calls light cues and sound cues, orders the sets changed, the curtains opened or closed, and cues actors, singers, and dancers to make entrances.

Prior to a performance, he announces "Half-hour" back-stage (half an hour before curtain time, at which time all per-formers must have signed in as "present,"), "Fifteen minutes," "Five minutes," and then, "Places, please." If a performer he expects to be standing by is not there he will call for that per-son over the backstage sound system (if one exists), or send an assistant hurriedly to fetch him.

The production stage manager nightly dispatches the or-chestra into the pit—probably five minutes before curtain, al-lowing the members time to "tune up." He also sends the con-ductor to start the overture just prior to beginning the show.

Backstage conduct is the responsibility of the production stage manager. Before every performance, a roster of the cast members is posted just inside the stage door. Each performer must sign in not later than "half-hour." The production stage manager removes the sheet at half-hour. Anyone who comes in afterwards must go to the stage manager and explain the cause of tardiness. If someone is five to ten minutes late, there is general concern because the role that the absentee plays—small or large—must be filled. An assistant stage manager will try telephoning the absentee, since he may have overslept, or met with an accident, and so forth.

In any theater, time is a very personal thing. Stars gener-ally allow themselves at least one hour. Every professional dancer is "in" an hour before performance in order to spend as much time as needed to warm up.

In the nonprofessional theater, experienced directors tell me that half an hour is insufficient time for the performers to ready themselves. Therefore, each nonprofessional theater backstage should be scheduled strictly on the basis of how familiar the performers are with using stage makeup, how long it takes them to dress, and whether or not there will be a group vocal and dance warm-up before the cast is ready to perform. However long these procedures take should determine the time set for arriving at the theater, making liberal allowance for accomplishing everything. That set time, whether half-hour, an hour before curtain, or even longer, must be strictly enforced.

Tardiness in the theater is a serious matter. If any performer in a professional production arrives later than the designated hour three times, he may be dismissed. If this seems rash, I can assure the reader that it is not. Discipline in theater is more essential than in the army. If one actor can bend the rules as he wishes, then everyone else can, and there will be no way to secure the regularity of a performance. An actor, singer, or dancer need give only three hours maximum to a performance. If he is unable to comply with this rule of punctuality, which applies to everyone, he simply should not be in the theater, whether on a professional or a nonprofessional level.

In the professional theater, everyone has an understudy. If a performer is not present and on time, the understudy will be surrounded at once with a wardrobe person making alterations in a costume, the stage manager rehearsing lines, the musical director reminding him of a song, a dance captain reviewing some steps, and so on, until curtain time. If the missing performer should show up, there will be relief and fury. If he fails to appear, apprehension will intensify.

In the nonprofessional theater, understudies are not generally used, and to me this is a dangerous practice. On Broadway, understudies are essential. People outside the cast are seldom used. (If one outsider understudies a star, he is called a "standby.") Instead, it is common practice to designate certain people within the cast and ensemble to rehearse and take over one or as many as three parts in case of an emergency. It is only a shifting, but the practice requires more rehearsal time.

(Some time ago I directed a version of *The Beggar's Opera* that I had made. On the very day of the first performance, the leading actor was sent to a hospital and I had to rehearse someone else [William Eythe] for 48 hours, using the rest of the cast for half of that time. We were delayed two days in opening.)

A good production stage manager earns the respect of the people who work under him. He is *not* good if he indulges in rages, or becomes too "personal" with people who must take his orders. He is the connecting link among the stage director, authors, choreographer, and the performers.

A celebrated director once decided, a few minutes before a performance, to cut out a line of dialogue. He went directly to the star's dressing room and made his decision known to her alone. The line happened to be a cue for a change in lighting. As the time for the cue passed without the lines being spoken, the stage manager was naturally a little late in calling the change. Puzzled, he asked the star afterward if she had forgotten the line and was told that the director had cut it– without informing the production stage manager. There was a violent argument later and the director could only offer humble apologies.

When the director has completed his job, the production stage manager is at the head of the show, making every effort to maintain the show's original shape. He is Jupiter; he spends the performance hours standing behind a narrow desk, among wires and ropes; he slaves and is respected. But he remains unknown.

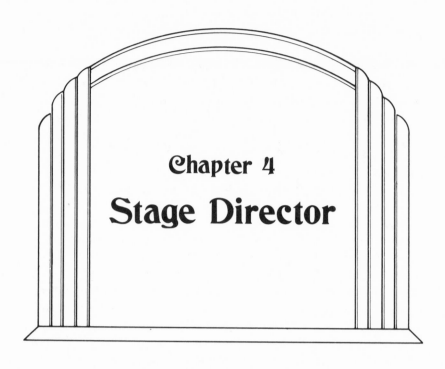

Chapter 4

Stage Director

IT SHOULD BE STATED at the outset of this chapter that *all* thea-ters—professional or nonprofessional—are necessarily differ-ent from one another. In the nonprofessional theater, the dif-ference is first due to geography, that is, the distance away from a larger center where trained personnel exist. Some-times these people can be persuaded (available funds create a second difference) to participate in a production. However it has to be accomplished, the best *possible* production must be created. No one can ask for anything more. Producer and stage director may necessarily be roles wrapped into the body and mind of a single person. When human resources are strictly limited, enthusiasm can unearth all kinds of unex-pected help from others. The leader—producer, director, or whatever title he bestows on himself—must believe that he is going to create the best show imaginable. If this sound like

Pollyanna, then so it does! But such an attitude set against what appear to be overwhelming odds is what turns trash cans into Greek columns, two lights into a sun-flooded tropical island, a dress made of cheesecloth into a coronation robe, and a young girl who studied ballroom dancing as a child into the much-needed choreographer. "More" is not always better—by a long shot. While experience is desirable, it has to be gained somewhere. Necessity coupled with enthusiasm can create almost anything, provided a few basic principles are understood, and simplicity can be far more effective in any good production than all the equipment and hoopla on Broadway!

The stage director is the artistic head of the production. He is chosen by the producer (or he may also *be* the producer) because of his background, his experience with musical shows, the quality of his leadership, and his human ability to collaborate with the many creative people on the one hand and the performers on the other.

A stage director—even one generally considered excellent—should ideally have had experience with musical shows if that is what he is engaged for, because he must know about many things that do not exist in nonmusical theater. In the matter of casting, he should be able to decide whether he will be dealing primarily with singers, or with actors who can sing. The difference between the performers in these two categories is enormous.

In a musical such as *The Most Happy Fella,* for example, Tony and Rosabella must have well-developed singing voices. Tony is a robust high baritone (nearly operatic) and Rosabella is a lyric soprano. Cleo and Herman are typical musical comedy singers, as is Joey. This mixture of vocal requirements is unusual in the average musical show. Today's young people seriously interested in musical theater have usually studied singing, dancing, acting, and speech. So many of them are eager to be cast in a show that, from the many who turn out to audition, the requirements of the various roles can usually be satisfied.

If the stage director is casting a musical comedy with less demanding vocal requirements and a greater dependence on acting style, he should view the needs of the particular role in proper perspective. For example, the leading male role in Frank Loesser's *How To Succeed in Business Without Really Trying* is an engaging young man, a *farceur* who can get by with less than a great voice. The songs are not demanding vocally but the role must be acted with style, charm, and wit.

Very often the clue to what is needed—or where the casting accent is to be placed—can be determined by a glance at the original Broadway cast. On Broadway, the director has the widest possible choice of performers, especially in casting leading roles. The "clues" are easy to follow. If Ray Bolger was the star, the role is primarily a dancing one. If Robert Morse *(How To Succeed)* played the lead, it is chiefly for a comic actor. If Ezio Pinza played the part, the role certainly required expert singing.

This business of proper casting is important, though not the principal function of the stage director. Before he undertakes his position, the stage director should have a production "concept" firmly in mind, and he must feel a great sense of empathy with the project as a whole.

This question of concept is difficult to explain, since it means many different things to different people. Jerome Robbins had the initial concept for *West Side Story:* he based it on *Romeo and Juliet,* yet he combined certain characters, and made the struggle that originally existed between two families—the Montagues and Capulets—a conflict between young Puerto Ricans and young "white" Americans, set in New York in the recent past.

While Robbins' concept of *West Side Story* was at the core of *creating* the show, many stage directors dealing with a revival may also have concepts that provide added freshness without distortion. At the same time, the stage director should not be given license to impose a concept that is untrue to the basic material, and therefore a misinterpretation of the authors' ideas. Orson Welles, many years ago, did memorable productions (nonmusical) of two of Shakespeare's plays: *Macbeth* and *Julius Caesar.* Among the thorniest problems for any stage director dealing with *Macbeth* are the scenes involving the witches. They are difficult to conceive and execute, stage-wise. What should they look like, sound like, and so forth? The

40

witches have sometimes been cast as men. Their cauldron has been stylized so that they stare into light rather than a gypsy-like kettle. Welles envisioned the play (despite the Scottish names of the characters) as taking place in Haiti. The struggle for power, the intense play of ambitions are historically applicable to Haiti's past. What made the witches easier to deal with was Welles' treating them as voodoo people—indigenous to the strange island. The concept worked without distortion of Shakespeare's original.

Welles' production of *Julius Caesar* was in what was then "modern dress" during the very real war against Fascism! Shakespeare's Romans became Italian mobsters. They wore long topcoats and wide-brim hats, pulled down over their brows at a menacing angle. Shakespeare's theme was instantly clearer to the audience of the thirties. The play was not distorted but clarified.

You're a Good Man, Charlie Brown was originally directed by Joseph Hardy. Since he was dealing with children and "Snoopy," a dog, and the production could not utilize either, the director had to substitute imagination for reality. The scenery consisted of "forms," blocks of varying bright colors and shapes that were moved about by the performers to represent anything called for by the play. The props followed the same nonrealistic pattern. Audiences comprehended.

There is usually a variety of choices (concepts) the stage director can utilize. He can set his show in a period different from the one the author indicated. He can stylize the action, removing it from "pure" reality. Especially in a revival, he is free to make any changes in production (although *not* in the script, music, or lyrics) that do not distort the original.

The stage director must work with department heads who will share his concept and help him to make it work. The stage director will need their help and cooperation and must be sure that they will provide him with artistic assistance and a feeling of supportive cooperation.

At *all* rehearsals, the stage director is the boss. He will have (aided by others) worked out a realistic schedule that will allow him to accomplish what must be done within the allotted time. While he will want as much time as possible for his own work of directing the libretto, for possibly staging some or all of the nondanced musical numbers, and for integrating all the parts into a whole, he must allow necessary working hours to the choreographer and the musical director so that they can prepare their own elements. Without these, the stage director will be unable to put together a musical show, which is, after all, a play with songs and dances.

The rehearsals should be preceded by weeks of discussion among all department heads so that the stage director can define exactly what he hopes to achieve. Each department head will be able to discuss his own problem in relation to this concept and what his needs are in terms of time and personnel.

Rehearsals, whether on Broadway or in the regional theater, are to be planned and used precisely as something precious and never-to-be-wasted. What too many people—directors in particular—do not seem to realize is that, in scheduling practice time for a musical show, it is possible and necessary to have *several* rehearsals going on simultaneously. Sometimes, for maximum effect, one or another of the directors will need to make small sacrifices: giving up one or two people for a part of one rehearsal because they are more important in another that is scheduled at the same time.

For example, let us consider rehearsals for *My Fair Lady*. The following is a list of all of the musical numbers (we will *not* forget the spoken scenes):

ACT I

1. Street Entertainers (3 dancers) (Passersby, unidentified personnel of all classes who "dress" the stage without detracting from the dance trio)
2. "Why Can't the English?" (Higgins) (Both Pickering and Eliza speak during the song and a cockney sings a bit)
3. "Wouldn't It Be Loverly?" (Eliza and male quartet)
4. "With a Little Bit of Luck" (Doolittle, Harry, and Jamie)
5. "I'm an Ordinary Man" (Higgins)
6. "With a Little Bit of Luck" (reprise) (Doolittle with chorus—for the first time—of males and females)

42

7. "Just You Wait" (Eliza)
8. "The Rain in Spain" (Higgins, Eliza, and Pickering)
9. "I Could Have Danced All Night" (Eliza, Mrs. Pearce, and two maids)
10. "Ascot Gavotte" (Male and female chorus)
11. "On The Street Where You Live" (Freddy)
12. "The Embassy Waltz" (Higgins, Eliza, Karpathy, and all dancers)

ACT II

1. "You Did It" (Higgins, Pickering, Mrs. Pearce, and small mixed chorus of servants)
2. "Just You Wait" (reprise) (Eliza)
3. "On The Street Where You Live" (reprise) (Freddy), going into:
4. "Show Me" (Freddy and Eliza)
5. "The Flower Market" (Eliza and male chorus)
6. "Get Me to the Church on Time" (Doolittle, Jamie, Harry, male chorus, then mixed chorus, dancers)
7. "A Hymn to Him" (Higgins, with spoken interjections from Pickering)
8. "Without You" (Eliza and Higgins)
9. "I've Grown Accustomed to Her Face" (Higgins)

This "program" shows an unusually small employment of singing and dancing ensemble, although there are quartets, duets, and other small ensembles taken from (in the original production) 16 singers and 20 dancers. Also, it should be noted that many of these played minor speaking parts. In addition, many members of the ensemble are moved about stage (to "dress" it) although they neither sing nor dance in these "crossover" moments.

In drawing up rehearsal schedules, since both ensemble groups (male and female) have such a small amount of music to learn, and the dancers have but a few "dances," it seems clear that so many were employed because of the need for their *physical* presences in at least five scenes. The musical director would need less time with the vocal ensemble than is usual, and the choreographer, with only three important dances, would have more than customary time to spend assisting the stage director with large scenes and with the difficult staging of musical numbers.

On the other hand, in the case of *My Fair Lady,* the stage director will be unusually busy. After scene 1, there are (in scene 2) only four characters and three offstage voices used briefly.

Scene 3 uses four principals and contains a simple solo song.

Scene 4 is very brief and uses three choruses, including a reprise of a song ("With a Little Bit of Luck") from scene 2.

Scene 5 uses four principals and a short chorus of servants (perhaps six singers) plus "The Rain in Spain" and "I Could Have Danced All Night," the former a trio of principals and the latter a solo with two female chorus members and Mrs. Pearce.

Scene 6 is brief, is performed by three actors (one is Mrs. Higgins' chauffeur, who speaks only one line), and has no song.

Scene 7, the big Ascot scene, employs the entire ensemble (singing and dancing) and seven actors.

Scene 8 is brief, has the lovesick Freddy, a policeman, and Mrs. Pearce.

This pattern of small scenes utilizing few actors, with occasional larger scenes that employ singers and dancers, is also the pattern of Act II. Because of the small cast, Higgins, Eliza, and Pickering are in constant demand at rehearsals.

In reviving *My Fair Lady,* there should be little conflict among the three departments that must collaborate in order to produce the musical show as a complete entity.

Oklahoma!, on the other hand, has nine real principals and fourteen other performers who play small parts and are taken from the ensemble. Scene 1 is long and contains:

1 duet

1 solo with ensemble dancing

1 solo

1 vocal chorus

44

1 solo, with female chorus and a dance

1 solo, with male chorus and a dance

1 duet

This abundance of singing and dancing shared by the entire company is more common in musical shows than is the pattern indicated in *My Fair Lady*. More singing and dancing means a greater number of separate rehearsals, and this kind of show is more difficult for the stage director, who must content himself with allowing the nonspeaking (musical) portions to dominate rehearsal time.

In addition to his dealings with performers, the stage director needs to approve—in fact, often suggests—the scenery he wants for his production. The scene and costume designers consult as to color and style and then have consultations with the stage director and lighting designer.

Lighting is of great importance in both Broadway and nonprofessional theaters (see Chapter 9). On Broadway, where the show is to be brought into theaters containing no lighting equipment, the lighting designer has to work out a draft that resembles an architect's plan. He orders the number of lighting instruments, amount of connective wire, boxes of colored gelatins, and switchboards that he has determined to be necessary.

In the nonprofessional theater, where most often the instruments and switchboards exist permanently, the lighting designer's problem is to find out from the stage director, the script, and the choreographer what is essential, and then to rehang and focus lights and install the colored gelatins he requires.

The stage director cannot merely *reproduce* a show he remembers seeing some time ago, even if that other production represented perfection for him. The director is a creative person in his own right and he will utilize the present differences to his own advantage. The principals will be less experienced, less mature. The dancers will be younger and less technically proficient. Many of the singers may have voices equal to those in the original ensemble but will nevertheless lack the experience. The orchestra players, stagehands, and designers will not rival the expertise of the original. The director faces different challenges, not with discouragement but with understanding. The director must inspire his cast to perform as well as they are capable of performing. The entire production needs to be geared so that audiences will not make comparisons with the original production but will be able to enjoy what is given them now. At any rate, memories are too often inaccurate). Even on the highest professional level, one cannot refuse to see *Hamlet* because one once saw it performed by, for example, Sir John Gielgud!

The cast, whatever their capabilities, are the raw material with which the director works, and must be molded into a convincing and enjoyable ensemble.

$$* \qquad * \qquad *$$

It is usual that, at the first meeting of the entire company, the show is read aloud by the members of the cast—each character reading his own part. If the principals have already learned their solos, they will sing. Otherwise, a pianist will play a musical number or perhaps the director or the musical director will sing it! The first read-through serves a dual purpose. It gives the stage director some idea of the quality of potential interplay among the members of his cast and it will fascinate all the participants to hear the entire show, providing an incentive for them. Of course, the dances will not have been put into rehearsal and they will necessarily be omitted on this first day (although the music for them may be played).

After this reading, the stage manager (see Chapter 3) will announce a schedule for the balance of the day. It is always wisest to permit the singers, dancers, and principals to do their individual work first. Then the stage director will be able to work on the scenes leading up to and following each completed number.

Many different directors follow many different procedures after the cast reading. Some begin immediately to block (place the actors in desirable positions on the imaginary set and tell them where and how to move, sit, stand, etc.), as much as time allows. I should think that this way is preferable for a director working with inexperienced nonprofessional performers. Another type of director explains the set-that-is-to-be, discusses the characters, and lets the actors improvise their movements in the scene. After that, this director discusses the things he liked about what he saw and the many things he took exception to which, in his opinion, would not work. Then, selecting what he liked, perhaps with modifications and clarifications, he proceeds to block the scene, including the elements he favored. This method is more time consuming than the first but it has this to recommend it: the director will have seen a kind of "free" expression of the performers that may stimulate his own imagination. He will see something fresh and previously unthought of, and from this he may derive some ideas—perhaps not exactly what he saw—that would never have otherwise occurred to him.

As the show proceeds in rehearsal, he will usually run several scenes in sequence without interfering with them, then give notes and corrections.

The songs in a good musical should come at moments of some kind of climax. They occupy precisely the same position in their shows that Shakespeare's soliloquies do in his plays. The performers should have learned their songs prior to the start of stage rehearsals and, when the songs occur, they should be staged so that what precedes and what follows in the scene leads up to them and melds into speech as soon after as possible.

Of course, the songs should have been staged separately and precisely so that, when they are included in the scene, they will constitute a large piece—previously missing—in the jigsaw puzzle.

If the libretto (book) of a musical functions properly, it will *rely* on the music and, often, on the dancing; the show should not exist without these elements. The songs—when they are functional—will clarify the character and/or emotions of the singer to the audience, or lead the show ahead. (If a song literally *stops* a show, it has simply been put there to no purpose.) Two examples of "functional" songs follow.

In Lynn Riggs' play *Green Grow the Lilacs*, the character of the villain, Jeeter, is rather two-dimensional: he is filthy, filthy-minded, psychotic, and horrific. He is not a human being and he evokes no sympathy from the audience. However, in *Oklahoma!*, the musical version of that play, Rodgers and Hammerstein give him a song ("Lonely Room") in which he explains his misery, his quite normal desire for a girl and *this* girl in particular; deplores his loneliness; and finally, resolves to do something about his situation. He is then a *man* with understandable appetites and frustration. The song elucidates the character and gives him another dimension.

In *Guys and Dolls*, "I'll Know" is an angry conversation between the hero and heroine. It grows out of the preceding scene, develops it, and, by the conclusion of the song, the two characters are "set," dramatically, in concrete blocks.

Anything—*anything*—in the book or music or lyrics of a musical that is not functional simply does not belong. However, in the nonprofessional theater, where most musicals that are produced have already been worked on, torn apart, and put together—usually improved—the director needs to assess the function of the scenes and songs as they exist, and stage them so that their purposes are understood and the many parts of the show are seen in their true proportions.

No director should insist on giving a "line reading" (a specific manner of speaking a sentence) to an actor unless the actor's own reading demonstrates beyond any reasonable doubt that he fails to comprehend the meaning of the lines. Nor should the director insist on a characterization without first observing the actor's own tendencies. If the director *does* insist, he will not get from the actor what this particular person has to give; instead, he will be superimposing his own ideas. In the end, this may be better, but there is always a danger that the director's idea is based on a memory of another—perhaps the original—production and what he seeks is mimicry rather than acting.

This method of re-creation in summer musical stock companies is often a poor compromise but quite understandable when a company has slightly less than a week to rehearse an entire show. In many cases the leads have done their roles previously, either on Broadway, on tour, or in other companies. Quite naturally, they want to *recall* precisely what they did before, and many of them will attempt to take the direction out of the hands of the director in order to instruct another performer as to how and where something is to be done.

Time is so abbreviated that there is no possibility of "creating" a performance and, under such conditions, the local director must be content to accept from principals experienced in playing the roles whatever they have been accustomed to doing. The local director will then assume the role of "traffic cop," attempting to prevent collisions. This sort of situation—summer stock—finds the stage director in his least attractive and least authoritative position.

Lest the reader get an erroneous impression of my own point of view, let me say clearly that, under usual circumstances (which summer stock is not), I would resent anyone's usurping the director's authority. I recall once attending a first rehearsal of a play in which Sir John Gielgud was both directing and acting. He had done this play many times before as an actor in various roles, and as director. Many of the performers had played in the same play, in their same parts, and under the direction of Sir John. At the very outset, one actor addressed the director, reminding him of the way he had done this scene previously. Sir John replied without animus that what the actor referred to was done in *that* production, but that *this* one was *this* one and everyone in it should forget anything he had ever done before! There were no similar interruptions or suggestions.

In regional productions or in schools where all of the performers look to the director for guidance, the director behaves in much the same way as his Broadway counterpart. He has prepared himself to do what is needed far ahead of rehearsals and has brought together the cast and company that, in his own opinion, is the best available. He must always remember that theater, especially musical theater, is not and cannot be *democratic*. One does not take a vote on what is right or wrong. There can be only one voice, one vision, one authority that controls everything and everybody—the director.

Since he is human, he may make mistakes, but he also must

be honest and acknowledge that what he is doing in a particular scene or in handling a particular performer is incorrect because it is not working properly. In such cases he tries other ways. He has *private discussions* with an actor, or the producer, choreographer, stage manager, or musical director. He listens and reconsiders. He does not have to accept the ideas or suggestions given him, but he *must* listen and think. Perhaps there *is* a better way. If he truly thinks so, he will take that other way and give it a try. It also may not work, but he has a responsibility to continue working and trying until he is able to discover a way out of his difficulties.

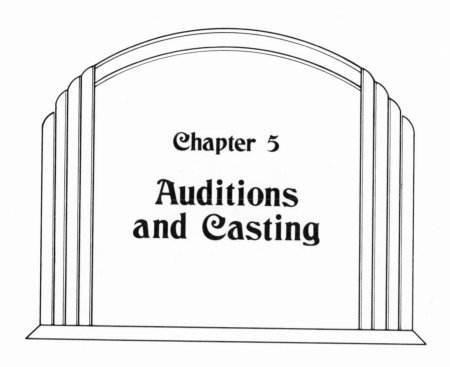

Chapter 5

Auditions and Casting

Now that you have chosen the show you wish to produce, and you have four essential department heads—stage director, choreographer, musical director, and stage manager—all of you must begin the arduous and often unpleasant job of casting the show. Prior to this you will have had many meetings and made collaborative decisions, discussed earlier. Some of the most important will concern casting—just whom do you want?

These decisions must be based on a number of considerations: the age and physical appearance of the principals to be cast, especially when they are playing opposite one another, their ability to sing the songs *as written* or *printed* in the vocal score, their credibility as actors, their ability to dance or at least move with some grace, and their "quality" for the various

226259

kinds of emotions they will be required to express in the particular show.

When these all-important decisions are made (usually with regard to four or more principals), it is necessary to consider the needs of the ensemble. (I have already pointed out the possibility, if such is desirable, of using more singers and dancers than are absolutely necessary.) The musical director should have studied the vocal score in order to determine the importance, vocally, of the singing ensemble. If they sing in unison (only one musical line that everyone sings together, as in *West Side Story*, for example), a few vocalists will suffice. If, on the other hand, the choruses are subdivided into four, five, or six parts (*Oklahoma!*, for example), the musical director will need eight to ten or twelve people in his ensemble. More would be more effective. Then—how *many* such numbers exist in the score? If there are only one or two and these seem unimportant, what is required of the singers can easily be reduced, even to performing a single line.

The stage director should be actively involved in these decisions since he may need more "bodies" on the stage for a variety of reasons. One or two people at a fair, or graduation, or in a mob scene would indeed be ridiculous!

Likewise, the choreographer should have studied the vocal score to determine the length and importance of the dances involving more than one or two people, the number of pieces to be choreographed, the style of the music, and the purpose of the dances. A summation of all of these will clarify, at least generally, the number of dancers needed.

You must—for a variety of reasons—begin with the selection of principals, especially the role that is largest, or most difficult to cast. Let us take several specific examples.

The first is *Wonderful Town*, based on *My Sister Eileen*. The leading character is the older sister, Ruth. Because of her protective, suspicious nature, she inclines toward caution and hardness. She is a comedienne. She is not an ingenue and must be a strong contrast to her foolish, naïve young sister Eileen, who believes everyone, is adventuresome, and would be in constant difficulty were it not for Ruth. Maturity versus immaturity is the essential theme in the casting of these two parts.

Ruth's vocal demands (she was played originally by non-singer/comedienne Rosalind Russell) are limited. She has one comedy solo, "A Hundred Easy Ways To Lose A Man," which relies on the lyrics rather than the music for its effectiveness. She sings (or howls) a duet ("Ohio") with her sister. Another duet with Eileen, "Wrong Note Rag," is fast, humorous, and, again, relies on vigorousness and fun rather than any vocal polish. There are other musical participations for Ruth but all of them require very limited vocal ranges (about five notes!) and few of them entail "singing." Ruth also has two simple singing dances that depend on no particular dance technique. Instead, they are rhythmic without being dance-like.

What does all of this add up to? Ruth Sherwood, the leading role in *Wonderful Town*, is chiefly a comedienne, an actress ideally in her early thirties with a feeling for song and dance, if not great skill in those techniques. If the actress selected for this part can execute these needs, the show should be a big success.

Second, let us examine the leading character in a quite different musical show: *Gypsy*. It was originally played (and sung) by Ethel Merman; little else need be said. Rose is the mother of two daughters who become young adults during the show—a fact that more or less sets her age. She is brash and energetic. As Arthur Laurents' book is literate and Rose's character is well defined, she must act. More than anything else however, she must sing!

There are many kinds of singing. Without going into technical discussions, let me cite some examples of very different roles. There are Mimi in Puccini's *La Bohème*, Brünnhilde in Wagner's *Die Walküre*, Queen of the Night in Mozart's *The Magic Flute*, Rosalinda in Strauss' *Die Fledermaus*, Marietta in Herbert's *Naughty Marietta*, Eliza Doolittle in Loewe's *My Fair Lady*, and so on.

Probably none of the ladies capable of singing these roles would be musically satisfying in the role of Rose in *Gypsy*, although all of them might sing conventionally much, much better, especially in the view of voice teachers. Rose has many great Styne-Sondheim songs to sing, including "Some People," "Let Me Entertain You," "Everything's Coming Up Roses," and "Rose's Turn." All of them are blockbusters and explode in their scenes, provided they are sung as character exclamations and not as beautiful songs—at least in a traditional sense. The proper delineation of Rose's character relies strongly on her dazzling delivery of these songs. As good as the show is, a timid or lyric-voiced Rose would spell disaster for the project.

The third example of principal selection is Sister Sarah in Frank Loesser's *Guys and Dolls*. (This show is different from all others in that all four leading characters—Sarah, Sky, Nathan, and Adelaide—are important and, although Sarah ends up with Sky, the leading man, it is Adelaide who is the female star.) Sarah is a kind of "Salvation Army" lassie. Cold at first, self-righteous, ignorant of the true ways of life, attractive, humorless, she is a "done to" rather than a "doer." However, she is the only one of the four principals who should have a "legitimate" (in this case, soprano) voice. Let us understand this term "legitimate" as I shall use it. The singer who possesses a legitimate voice has the *ability, technique,* and *training* to sing classical material. At the same time, she must also comprehend the style of the show so that "I'll Know," "If I Were a Bell," "I've Never Been In Love Before," and others will not make her sound like a recitalist, but a character in a contemporary show who understands the importance of rhythm and is not impeded by singing *bel canto*. The "beauty of singing" is superseded by the somewhat rough style of the libretto. Also, since Nathan and Sky will be basically actors rather than singers, and Miss Adelaide is a kind of "torch" singer, Sarah's vocal ability must not put her too far away from the others. It is possibly her "primness" more than anything else that defines her vocal characterization.

Fourth and last, let us consider together Julie Jordan and Billy Bigelow in Rodgers and Hammerstein's *Carousel*. While the show is based on a classic of the modern nonmusical theater, *Liliom* by Ferenc Molnar, as a musical it is as American as the original play is Hungarian. In casting this musical, it is absolutely essential that these two leading characters have voices with power, range, and all that is meant by "vocal control." Billy's big vocal piece is the "Soliloquy." He and Julie each sing "If I Loved You" and other big, romantic numbers. While acting is important, *Carousel* cannot be performed successfully without technically proficient singers. And, physically, Billy should be as large and somehow "menacing" as Julie is (seemingly) helpless.

It is interesting to note that in *Oklahoma!* the ballet (by Agnes deMille) that follows "Out of My Dreams" employed dancers as replacement for singers—dancers who "doubled" in the singers' roles—and that in *Carousel* the major dance ("Beach Ballet") is made for a young *dancer* who has to act, and sings only in ensemble.

In casting a show on Broadway, the musical director choosing singers and the choreographer selecting dancers will encounter any number of people who have worked for them previously. The reemployment of many of these same people can be helpful and can also become a great temptation, since the directors are familiar with their capabilities. There also exists a degree of personal relationship (rapport) that both directors find it difficult to break when they see someone newer and better, or find that some of the previously used performers can no longer equal their former performance level.

In the nonprofessional theater, the casting problem, partially due to the same conditions, seems to be at least equally complex. According to Jim Cavanaugh, associate professor at Mount Holyoke College in Massachusetts,

> actors whom the director has worked with before, now expect priority consideration, and backstage workers now expect it's their turn on stage. These factors are compounded when bringing other directors aboard, on a musical. For instance, the choreographer has worked with some of the dancers before, and likely has some of them in class. Surely, these will be some of the best dancers in town (or on campus) but just as surely they'll be known to some of the other people auditioning as proteges of the choreographer—a ripe situation for ill feelings that can (sometimes legitimately) harm the reputation of the theater. Further, the "best dancers in town" may be useless for anything but dancing.

The same problem occurs when a musical director has encouraged his/her students, or choir members, to come to auditions. And the complications increase when the girl with the loveliest voice is twice the size of the Eliza Doolittle the director has envisioned, and when the best actress can't possibly sing the role.

Let us examine additional casting considerations. If the leading lady you've cast is taller than average, you might want to follow the Broadway example of making her look more petite by casting a fairly tall ensemble. If she's not as young as the role specifies, the ensemble, too, might consist of mature singers and dancers.

A short leading man, while not unheard of, especially if he possesses the musical and acting abilities, could be made to look more towering by surrounding him with even shorter ensemble members.

Small parts are usually played by members of the ensembles. The stage director will have the singers and dancers read, taking special note, as in any audition, of those who look physically like the characters he is trying to cast. Generally, however, members of the ensemble will be cast on the basis of their primary ability, with acting becoming a consideration only in this later phase.

Another problem to be taken into serious consideration, especially by producers in the nonprofessional theater, has to do with the *keys* in which the songs appear. Now this explanation can be complex, and I urge the reader to follow carefully.

If the show you are planning to do is *printed* in a *complete* vocal score (*not* "selections from" or sheet music of one or two separate songs), the keys appearing in the *vocal score* will be those of the orchestrations you are renting. It would be helpful if the musical director would examine the score to determine the *range* of the principals prior to auditions. If he has done this, he will provide himself with guidelines that will obviate arguments as to whether or not Agnes Jones can sing "Carrie."

The accompanying chart illustrates precisely the vocal range of each part as it appears in the published vocal score of *Carousel*.

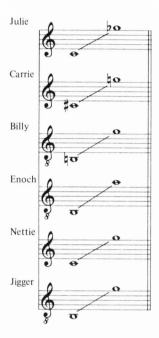

It will not be amiss if I explain just how these keys are arrived at. The composer of the show will have written the songs in whatever keys a singer can most comfortably perform them, or a key he particularly favors for each song. That initial key is seldom intended to be the final one. During the rehearsals of the original production, *all* keys of *all* songs are altered as necessary in order to accommodate the original performer. When the suitable key is arrived at through weeks of rehearsal, the orchestrator will make his arrangement accordingly.

To my knowledge, only Kurt Weill and Leonard Bernstein have not (certainly as a rule) changed keys. Both largely wrote music as they "heard" it, then cast *for the music.* This is not by any means a new procedure. In grand opera, composers wrote roles for definite singers who were able to negotiate the music. Occasionally Broadway composers have used this method. I have been told that Kurt Weill wrote *Lady in the Dark* for Gertrude Lawrence, whose vocal accomplishments were—to be kind—modest. There was one note in one song that she could not sing, and Weill altered the note but not the key of the song.

Be certain in casting your show that all your performers can comfortably negotiate the songs in the keys sent to you by the rental agency. Otherwise, you will have to transpose entire orchestrations to other keys, and there is more than a small chance that certain instruments will go out of their range—too high, or too low—and, in any case, the orchestration in another key will not sound as well as the original. The orchestrator of the original is, above all, a craftsman, and in making his arrangement he considers not only the character of the song and the singer's range, but precisely what is more effective and more easily negotiated for every single instrument of the orchestra. For example, the key of B major (5 sharps) creates problems for nearly everyone, and certain other keys are undesirable for the players of certain instruments.

With the passage of time, newly written shows tend to change not only in style, but in their requirements in terms of personnel. Sometimes this is evolutionary—a reaction against, or a growing out of, what has become "old." More often it is due to the shifting and now almost unbearable state of the economy.

The artistic result of this has been for some time to reduce the number of supporting people required—to simplify. For example, in *Oklahoma!* (1943) there were 16 well-trained singers and 16 extraordinary dancers. By the time of *West Side Story* (14 years later) Jerome Robbins used *no* singers but was able to find excellent dancers who were able to sing whatever was needed ("America," "Gee, Officer Krupke," "Tonight," etc.). By the time of Sondheim's *Company* (1970) there was a *single* dancer given one solo. Even before these latter two, *South Pacific* (1949) employed people who could act, sing loudly, and move. Joshua Logan, who directed it, also did what little choreography there was.

The recommendation I am trying to make in relation to the nonprofessional theater is that the requirements of the show be studied carefully prior to casting, since no two shows (after about 1950) are alike in their needs.

Today, *I Love My Wife* has a cast of four and a "combo" of four, also on stage. The *Chorus Line* company sings, dances, and acts. *I Do! I Do!* had a cast of two. Rodgers' *I Remember Mama* had no ensemble. *The Madwoman of Central Park West* (also a musical) had a cast of one.

There is also the consideration of types and ages. This, too, differs from show to show, and always has. Gilbert and Sullivan created their operettas so that members of their permanent company played similar roles with similar ranges in many of the shows, which is one reason why they are ideal as repertory pieces. The hero is a tenor; the heroine, a soprano; the "character lady" (Ruth in *Pirates*, Katisha in *The Mikado*, etc.) is a contralto; the leading comedian can sing quick "patter" songs clearly; and so on.

Lady in the Dark required a singing ensemble of boys and girls who had cultivated voices, looked attractive, and appeared not more than 21. *Best Foot Forward* needed young people of college age who could carry a tune and move. *Wonderful Town* needed "character" types in the singing ensemble since the men had to double as policemen, and the girls had to be more or less mature. Older men and women sang in *The Music Man* and in *My Fair Lady*.

In our time, "dinner theaters" have sprung up in many towns and cities, especially outside New York City. Some of these perform reduced versions of musicals, involving major cuts in the libretto; also, where ensemble singing is required, a quartet replaces what originally were four times that number of singers. This same practice can be applied, when needed, to nonprofessional theater.

*   *   *

Early in my career as musical director of shows and operas (now totaling 170), I was accustomed to hearing every singer who came to audition. This was time-consuming for me as well as for those hundreds of singers awaiting their turn.

I soon realized that hearing people sing who were physically wrong for the role—whether or not they had the greatest voices in the world—was a useless exercise, and decided never again to listen to anyone physically unacceptable for the particular show.

I cannot think that the nonprofessional theater would hold auditions vastly different from those to which I have grown accustomed. Prior to my casting *Lady in the Dark,* I heard everybody who wished to be heard. When I was charged to select only "people who looked no older than 21" and had pretty or handsome faces and good bodies, I began to eliminate the older and less attractive, fat and emaciated ones first. This procedure is known as "typing out," i.e., eliminating those who are not the right physical type. Then I heard the remaining people sing. (Incidentally, I learned that the physically attractive ones as a whole performed no better than others—singing included.)

The staff that hears auditions in the nonprofessional theater could prevent a great deal of personal embarrassment from its own as well as the audtionees' side if physical options were stated at the outset, and the *impossible* applicants were eliminated before singing or dancing tests. The people who are to be eliminated can be spoken to singly and in private to avoid anger and embarrassment.

Recently I had occasion to see a new show produced nonprofessionally in the middle west. There were good things about many performers and parts of the show. However, the entire project was rendered silly because the leading man *looked* 14 (he was actually 20), and he played against a girl who was clearly a woman. Neither he nor the show could be taken seriously.

Getting back to my auditions, once the "bodies" had been selected for singing, I heard them in any sequence: usually I asked them to sing eight bars of a ballad that showed off their voices, and sometimes after that I asked for eight bars of a rhythm song. Those people who seemed to be within the realm of possibility I alerted to return to final auditions. At these last auditions, I heard first *only* sopranos (in order to be able to contrast their voices), then altos, tenors, and baritones (basses). I never dismissed anyone until selections had been made—not final selections, but the more desirable possibilities.

Before those eliminated at this point were dismissed, the stage manager made careful record of their names, addresses, and telephone numbers, and noted that they were "alternate" choices. Many times, needing 16 singers, we ended up with 30 desirables (out of perhaps 80 at the finals), and then the final selections were made during much discussion by the musical director, stage director, and choreographer.

When I liked one voice particularly well, the choreographer had her or him waltz with the stage manager, or sometimes simply walk across the stage. Often there was bargaining. I would insist on certain people because their very large voices would help to create musical climaxes. The choreographer and stage director would agree, *provided* I would accept so-and-so who was an expert dancer or a strong actress.

There is an unfortunate feeling on the part of people who audition (less so on the part of those who listen), when they are not selected, that they have been treated unfairly, or that life is hopeless for the underdog. In my own experience, both attitudes are totally incorrect. It is not possible for those who audition to know precisely what is needed—vocally, physically, and in relation to others in the cast. Also, what is heard in a theater is far different from what is heard in a room—a more confined space. Then, too, voice teachers and parents can all too often be unrealistic, and the singer can be brainwashed into thinking she is not only better than she is, but better than everybody else.

As for the "underdog" attitude, it is equally unreal. I believe singers who go to auditions should *never* labor under the conviction that they are definitely going to be selected. Instead, I have always suggested that they do the very best they can without expecting anything. If they are selected, that's a happy surprise. *All* people go through the experience of being rejected from time to time. Rejection at an audition is no proof of failure. For example, I would never select Alfred Drake for an ensemble! His voice was a "personality" voice, and as Curly in *Oklahoma!* he was superb. In an ensemble, he would have been nonblending. Rejection at an audition is not the conclusion of anything, only the end of a single exploration.

Another word to those who would audition. Bring along

several contrasting songs so that the musical director—if he feels undecided about you on hearing one song—can hear another. *Listen to directions.* If you are asked to sing only the last eight bars of a ballad, do just that. Don't try to generate interest by choosing an unknown song or an aria from an obscure opera; the listener will be far more interested in *what* you are singing and, in the end, will not have heard your voice at all. Dress simply and don't try to be impressive by wearing a costume and an abundance of make-up that will appear gross without proper lighting, which you can depend on *not* getting. Be as relaxed as possible, and as pleasant and courteous. Remember that the listener is not enjoying this grueling task any more than you are. He will thank you (perfunctorily, to be sure) at the finish and it will make you more impressive if you will, in turn, thank him.

When it is your turn to sing, be certain that the sheet of music you give the accompanist is in the correct key for you. Don't expect him to be able to transpose just anything at sight. Sometimes he can, sometimes he cannot. Avoid lengthy musical introductions that serve no purpose as far as hearing your voice is concerned—this is not a recital but an audition. Only *how* you sing is of any interest to the auditioner.

To the musical director who will be listening: remember that the singer is nervous. Be helpful by your attitude. You will perhaps be bored, but that fact must have no bearing on this moment. You *need* the personnel you are in search of. Keep reminding yourself of the fact that this is indeed a search and not a time-wasting chore.

The final warning to everyone auditioning any kind of performer is that choices *must* be made on a level of ability and appropriateness for the specific show. Only the best and most useful should be selected. Any other consideration, if allowed to influence casting, can only be harmful to the project.

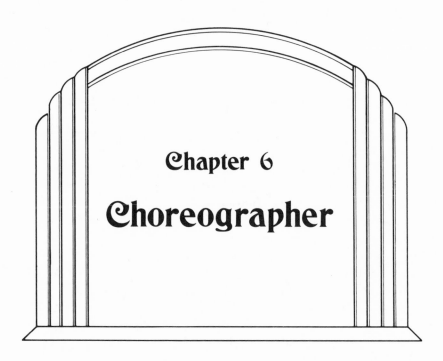

Chapter 6

Choreographer

AFTER WEEKS OF MEETING with the stage director and musical director, studying the score, and working with the scenic designer to perfect the sets, or parts of sets, in which dances will be taking place, the choreographer is ready for auditions.

Some choreographers prefer to begin by allowing each dancer auditioning to present a minute or minute-and-a-half dance that he or she has previously prepared, to show variety and skill, and to permit the choreographer to evaluate the dancer's maximum technique and style.

Whether or not the dancer has this option, the main part of all auditions is the same: repeating a "combination" or pattern of steps taught by the choreographer to small groups of auditioners at a time. After first learning the names of all dancers in the group (from their audition forms or by writing names down on the spot), the choreographer—or his assistant—will teach a simple combination, standing with his back to the dancers so they can observe from the perspective of the performer. He'll go through the combination several times, while the dancers behind him are learning it. Then he'll move away and they'll repeat it, possibly as a group, possibly singly or in twos and threes.

Perhaps several more combinations will be taught, growing in difficulty and complexity, until the choreographer has a good idea of which are the better dancers and, possibly more important, which are the better dancers for the style of this production.

The size of each group taught the combination depends on the size of the audition space, and the ability of the choreographer to observe and to learn names. Some are able to handle upwards of twenty at a time; some prefer no more than six or eight. Whatever works is valid, as long as everyone who wishes to audition can be accommodated within the hours, or days, allotted.

Then, in communion with the stage director and the musical director, the choreographer contributes to the casting of the play.

To approach the choreography of each number in a show in which the libretto is already set, the choreographer must be aware of what has preceded each dance and what will follow. He must know the music note for note and rhythm for rhythm. He will begin his precise planning several weeks before he starts to work with the dance group. For this planning stage, he will need a tape of the music and one or two dancers (one of them an assistant to the choreographer). During this period he will take one number at a time, thinking of the character of the people (whether they are Dutch painters, Japanese laborers, lords and ladies at a 16th-century court, "flower children," or any of a number of other kinds of people). Accordingly, before the rehearsals start, he will proceed to invent patterns of appropriate movement; these are then broken down into steps that are usually set to "counts," with the patterns containing the counted steps. At rehearsal, the dancers are taught the patterns, with the choreographer or his assistant calling the counts and the movements out loud; for example, "one, two, three, four; one, two, leap, four; one,

64

two, leap, four; turn around, left, four; walk right, three, four"; and so on.

Often when the musical phrases are evenly set in eight-bar patterns of 4/4 time, the counts go one, two, three, four, five, six, seven, eight; two, two, three, four, five, six, seven, eight; three, two, three, four, five, six, seven, eight; four, two, three, four, five, six, seven, eight. This amounts to 32 counts, or the eight musical 4/4 bars. It is then possible for the choreographer to speak of the "third 8," for instance, without starting each time at the beginning.

After the number has been completed and taught to the group of dancers, it is wise to repeat a finished dance on as many subsequent days as the schedule allows in order to keep it accurate, and to try to develop ease and a sense of style.

It is tremendously important that the choreographer do his "homework" prior to each scheduled meeting with the dance group. If he fails to do this, he will waste valuable time in rehearsal. On the other hand, he will earn the respect and gratitude of his dancers when they recognize the extent of his preparation and his direct ability to proceed to *rehearse* rather than painfully "create" while eight to twenty or more dancers stand about being bored.

In considering the kinds of dances he will do, it is well for the choreographer to evaluate the capabilities of his dancers. He must plan to do *only* those things that his dancers can encompass readily. It is more important that the dances be relevant to the style of the show, narrate clearly the scenario (when there is one), and reflect the spirit of that section, rather than be complex and beyond the ability of the dancers available to the choreographer. Simple is always better, to coin a phrase!

The job of the choreographer in the nonprofessional theater is infinitely less complex than that of his alter ego in the Broadway theater. The latter has to:

locate places in the script for the dances

create scenarios that continue a story line already set up

work with a dance arranger to create complementary music
bring into being a dance work that, in itself, has form

To put it simply, the choreographer of a new show has to have studied the libretto and the score so carefully that he locates one or two places where a dance work will enhance rather than interrupt the show. Then this dance has to be created with proper attendant music. Once it has been made, its length is always open to accusations of being "too long," in which case dance and music must be carefully cut so as neither to destroy the statement the dance has tried to make nor to annihilate the musical form.

Few of these issues will concern the nonprofessional choreographer. The show has been produced before. In most cases the vocal score (all of the songs with a piano part accompanying a vocal line) has been published. Unlike the cast album, where dance music seldom if ever appears, *all* of the dance music is included.*

It becomes the duty of the re-creating choreographer to study that music and discover how it fits into the libretto, who performs it, what leads up to it, and what happens afterward. Each of these issues is of vital importance.

While many dance numbers in older musical shows are pure entertainment "inserts," this style has become less prevalent in recent years. For the most part, dances in newer shows are integral parts of the show.

Sometimes the dance follows a song, or is inserted between vocal verses. To ascertain whether it exists only as entertainment, the choreographer should consult the original cast list. If the song preceding the dance was originally performed by Fred Astaire, Debbie Reynolds, or Ray Bolger, for example, you can be reasonably certain that this is a dance without scenario (it does not tell or continue a narrative), but is rather an

---

*Few composers write the dance music for their shows. Specialists called "dance arrangers" are engaged to write this music, drawing on themes from the main score. This task begins well before rehearsals start and continues until after the original production's out-of-town opening. The reason dance music rarely appears on an album is threefold: there is room for only a limited number of selections, and the public generally wants those with vocals; the chief composer wants all his own music and none of anyone else's on the album; and the dance music in most cases does not stand up alone, working only where needed—as a floor covering for the dance.

excuse to exploit the performer and to fulfill the audience's desire to see someone famed as a dancer exhibit his or her talents.

When the number is a "ballet" (a full-scale dance—not necessarily in ballet style), it undoubtedly is considered important, sometimes essential to the show as a whole, in the spot where it appears. The new choreographer must discover the *function* of such a dance so that it leads clearly out of what precedes it and makes its statement clearly in terms of movement. Although it probably has a definite ending, it should also act as a proper "set-up" for what follows it.

Several examples will serve as clarification. George Balanchine and Richard Rodgers created a "ballet" that tells a tale for Ray Bolger (an unusual use of this performer's talents) and Tamara Geva in *On Your Toes* (1936)—"Slaughter on Tenth Avenue." (Rodgers himself composed the music.)

For *The King and I,* Jerome Robbins created "The Small House of Uncle Thomas," which is an interpretation of *Uncle Tom's Cabin* done in an oriental manner with masks and props; at one point a width of blue-to-white material is "undulated" by 2 visible dancers from each side of the stage to represent the river. It has a political comment to make (the King is cruel and repressive although he admires President Lincoln's freeing of the slaves), and it parallels Eliza's attempt to escape with Tuptim's plans to elope with her lover despite the fact that she is one of the King's wives. In recreating this "ballet," the story must be clear and the style *suggestive* of oriental dancing. Although the essence of it is serious, what the audience sees is frequently amusing. Its relationship to the main line of *The King and I* should never be vague. At intervals in the ballet, a narrator explains in "broken" English what is going on.

Robbins also did an important and extremely funny ballet in which there is singing and speaking, a dream ballet that is a lie, in *Fiddler on the Roof.* The leading character, Tevye, has given his consent to the marriage of one of his daughters to a poor tailor, having previously consented to her marriage with a rich butcher—a widower. He is stumped for the way to tell his wife, Golde, of this change. While he is in bed with her he "creates" the people of a false dream, especially the dead wife of the butcher who threatens Tevye's daughter with frightening disaster is she marries the butcher.

There is great fun in the grotesqueness, and there is also a point. It leads to Golde's final conclusion that their daughter will *not* marry the butcher, thus realizing Tevye's intent in inventing the dream.

Agnes deMille created a ballet that ends Act I of *Oklahoma!*—a dream in which Laurey visualizes a fight over her between her real love, Curly, and Jud, the frightening hired hand. In the dream Curly is killed. She is awakened at the end of the dream by Jud, who is to accompany her to a picnic. She gives him her arm as she glances back to see a bewildered Curly wince and, not wishing to see her dream materialize, Laurey exits with Jud as Curly stands helpless and the curtain falls. The show cannot be performed without this ballet since it creates the situation that must be resolved in Act II.

There are many other ballets that tell stories pertinent to the shows that contain them. Some examples are:

"Beach Ballet" in *Carousel* (deMille)

"Mlle. Fifi" in *Look Ma, I'm Dancin'* (Robbins)

"Keystone Kops" in *High Button Shoes* (Robbins)

"Dance at the Gym" and "Somewhere" in *West Side Story* (Robbins)

Another classification of ballets entertains and fulfills purpose without furthering the plot of the show:

"Hernando's Hideaway" in *The Pajama Game* (Fosse)

"Steam Heat" in *The Pajama Game* (Fosse)

Different from those are the song-continuation dances:

"Get Me To The Church On Time" in *My Fair Lady* (Holm)

"Hey, Big Spender" in *Sweet Charity* (Fosse)

"Come to Me, Bend To Me" in *Brigadoon* (deMille)

"At The Ballet" in *A Chorus Line* (Bennett)

"Hello, Dolly!" in *Hello, Dolly!* (Champion)

Then there are semirealistic functional dance sequences:

"Funeral Dance" in *Brigadoon* (deMille)

"Sword Dance" in *Brigadoon* (deMille)

"Whip Dance" in *Destry* (Kidd)

"Punch and Judy Dance" in *Love Life* (Kidd)

"Tick-Tock" in *Company* (Bennett)

There are "entertainment" dances that were more common in earlier shows, but adapted as more functional in later ones:

"The Gladiola Girl" in *Lend an Ear* (Champion)

"Take Back Your Mink" in *Guys and Dolls* (Kidd)

"A Bushel And A Peck" in *Guys and Dolls* (Kidd)

Ballets in *Chicago* (Fosse)

Ballets in *Redhead* (Fosse)

Ballets in *New Girl in Town* (Fosse)

"The Beach Ball Ballet" in *No, No, Nanette* (Saddler)

"The Beardsley Ballet" in *Take Me Along* (White)

"Marian, the Librarian" in *The Music Man* (White)

"The Hero's Imagination" in *Irma la Douce* (White)

Most difficult to create and most important to the show as a whole is the opening number. It sets the mood and indicates the style of the show. An abstract dance (one that obviously exists for itself alone, without specific, easily communicated meaning) at the start of a show, when the characters have not yet been introduced and there is as yet no situation, gives the audience no "handle," no reason for being interested, and it usually fails.

Beginning a show with a meaningless dance is somewhat akin to the practices that were invariable in the early days of musical comedy, when the young, good-looking ensemble came out first, kicking with energy while they smiled, singing

69

a song that usually added nothing to the show. There was a purpose or two implicit in this formula: the audience was assured of the lovelies and of their liveliness, and their pointless exercises served to kill a bit of time before the stars were introduced, in order to allow for the noisy seating of latecomers. At the very least, what went on at the beginning of the show was pleasant, attractive, and energetic.

Today some misguided choreographers, unrestrained by higher authorities, occasionally begin a show with what amounts to strenuous calisthenics in an effort to show off the dancers and their own "creativity."

On the other hand, everyone agrees that knowing how to start a show is undoubtedly the rarest skill in all musical theater. There must be a "concept" that carries *into* the show and serves to establish time and/or place and provide for the introduction of plot, theme, and characters.

A few exceptional choreographic numbers—all of which include singing with lyrics that have definition—are the openings to:

A *Funny Thing Happened on the Way to the Forum* ("Comedy Tonight") (Robbins)

Wonderful Town ("Christopher Street") (Robbins)

Allegro ("Joseph Taylor, Jr.,") (deMille)

Company ("Company") (Bennett)

Once Upon a Mattress ("Many Moons Ago") (Layton)

Fiddler on the Roof ("Tradition") (Robbins)

Kiss Me, Kate ("Another Op'nin', Another Show") (Holm)

A Chorus Line (Bennett)

And there are others. All of these helped to lift the audience over the threshold of the show. Not self-indulgent, these openings worked hard and well to take us where we needed to be.

The styles of choreography are largely those of the creators of the dances, although they are colored by the music and

70

the character of the show. The theater itself uses everything it needs, regardless of origin, but these elements are adapted, not reproduced. In dancing today as always, ballet technique is the fountainhead—but no one would expect a performance of "Swan Lake" in *Guys and Dolls*! Most choreographers began working in various ballet classes, schools, and companies, but all of them have developed personal stamps that are clearly individual. Ballet is mixed with jazz, tap, "modern," ballroom, and other styles. In their application to the needs of the theater, they are never reproductions but are adaptations evolved from the imagination of the choreographer and utilized for the specific needs and purposes of the show.

As the choreographer usually also has to deal with nondancers on stage while the real ones dance, he has the options of positioning the nondancers about the stage, with instructions to watch the dance, or he can arbitrarily have them disappear off stage and return casually after the number.

Positioning nondancers on a stage while a dance is in progress will depend upon the locale in which the scene is taking place, the amount of space available for personnel not involved in the dance, and the nature of the dance itself. If, for example, the dance takes place in a saloon, there will be a bar and, if there is enough space, some small tables and chairs where the nonperformers can sit and perhaps be engrossed in drinking or conversation, with or without paying attention to the dancing, as the director wishes.

If it takes place in a palace ballroom, there may be a few chairs or a slightly higher stage level in the rear or on the sides. The placement or displacement of nondancers is not difficult, can be tried in a variety of ways at the last minute, used for color, or dispensed with altogether.

Many dance numbers, and dancing sequences in vocal numbers, are very long. Dance adds greatly to the artistry, the variety, the color of an evening in the theater, and, as stated, it often furthers the plot and/or the characterizations. However, it is no sacrilege to *cut* entire dances, or trim down, a little or a lot, dances or dance sequences that remain in the production. The original dance chorus had five weeks, of at least seven hours a day, to rehearse these dances. The choreogra-.

pher had nothing else to do, day and night, than prepare for rehearsal, and rehearse. The dancers were skilled professionals who had been dancing all their lives. Few of these conditions will exist in the nonprofessional theater, so there's no shame in cutting the material to fit the situation. If the leading lady is an expert singer but inept dancer, the original material is not so sacrosanct as to suffer from the elimination of the entire dance portion of her big song. If rehearsal time with chorus is limited, because of their outside commitments, for instance, it's foolish to try to stage several five-minute dances when *one* of them, well rehearsed, will be a show-stopper. It's pointless to force a chorus of good, but not excellent, dancers to present a seven-minute ballet, when trimming it to three will tighten the show, emphasize the good moments you do have, and not leave the audience wishing it were over. A few minutes with the musical director and the score, to assure yourselves that possible cuts won't make segues in the music ungainly or inartistic, a few minutes with the stage director to ascertain that he wasn't counting on that moment in that dance to show the couple falling in love, and an albatross of a nonworking dance can be transformed into a little jewel that represents the best work of choreographer and dancers alike.

When staging dances involving singers—or singing dancers—the choreographer must see that all who sing (particularly in solos and duets) face front as often as possible so that the audience can comprehend the lyrics and the performers can see the conductor. He must evaluate carefully the ability of singers to move: to what extent they can *really* dance, how they use their arms and hands, and the extent of their ability to coordinate physically.

If, for example, a male singer has, as they say, "two left feet," it is advisable that he move as little as possible without appearing to be a statue. In other words, musical staging must be a combination of the choreographer's or director's ideas with relation to the song and situation, and a careful tailoring of those ideas as they apply best to the performers' physical capabilities.

It is the choreographer's duty to go over scenic plans carefully so that he is assured of adequate floor space in which to work unhampered. Pillars, steps, furniture, and all other interfering objects should be done away with if possible. If such clearing of space is not possible, then the choreographer must recognize what he needs to accomplish despite their presence. If the dance is to be an important and developed one, the scene designer should cooperate and make every effort to clear the stage. If, on the other hand, the dance is small and unimportant and can be accomplished satisfactorily with only a few dancers, the choreographer should design his dances around the "objects" and, if possible, use them; otherwise the resultant physical awkwardness will be obvious to any audience, and the blame will probably fall on the choreographer.

In the nonprofessional theater the costumes should be designed and executed so that they do not interfere with the dancing. Further, with close cooperation between costume designer and choreographer, the lines of each costume will enhance the lines of the dance, and vice versa. Should the entire body be outlined with a tight-fitting garment? Should fringes, flounces, full skirts move in an interesting way as the dancers move? This relationship between choreographer and costume designer can make the dance better and the work of both artists—and the dancers themselves—more pleasing to the audience.

In dealing with the lighting designer, the choreographer would do well to remember that dance lighting is the latest art form in the theater. As stated earlier, most scenery for full dance numbers is the *absence* of scenery. The lighting designer is then lighting bare space and, with the choreographer, moving bodies and whatever combinations of bodies and space they can work out most artistically and to the point of the number's relation to the show. The sensitivity of this relationship can underscore more than any other the choreographer's visible contribution to the evening.

In certain shows of more recent vintage, where the dances are indigenous to the plot line, certain choreographers have copyrighted their dances. It is not necessary to discuss this at length, merely to point out that the book, music, and lyrics are also copyrighted. That information will be furnished along with everything else you need to know about the leasing of any material from the rental agencies.

It will interest some nonprofessional producers to know that it is possible to engage someone who assisted the original choreographer, or one of the original dancers who recalls the dances and has gone about recreating them in subsequent productions. Most leading Broadway choreographers have special, approved people they are in the habit of dispatching under such circumstances. I pass this on as information, since the local choreographer would not want to be slighted at bringing in an outsider, and the opportunity offered him to grow in each production should not be overlooked.

Addressing the least experienced choreographers, let me add a general word to remind them that a dance has form, that it passes through a series of designs, and that the "steps" given are in order to achieve these forms or designs and are not an end in themselves.

A last word about style versus content—in order to illustrate this, let me use an extravagant example. *A Funny Thing Happened on the Way to the Forum* is set in ancient Rome and the costumes conform to our idea of what the clothes would have been like in that time and place. The music, however, was composed by Sondheim only a few years ago, making no effort to imitate the music of ancient Rome. That is as it should be, since a contemporary show should be a product of its contemporary creators. The lyrics for "Comedy Tonight" are in English, not Latin. That being the case, there is no reason why the style of dancing—so long as it does no violence to the music and the libretto, which has a vaudeville or even burlesque quality (intentionally),—should not be the choreographer's own most comfortable style. Jerome Robbins' original dances reflected his style. Each choreographer approaching each number, must do it in line with his own talent and expertise. It might be a tap dance or a variety of other things. The point I want to make, however, is that it *should* represent the maximum talent and ability of the new choreographer doing what he can do best, given the group of dancers he has to work with.

74

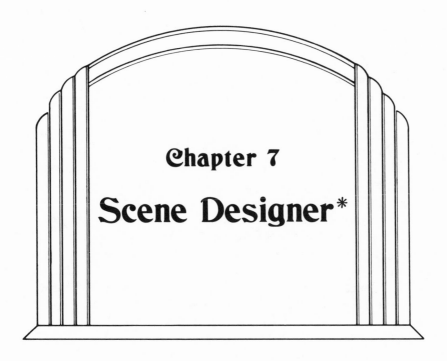

Chapter 7

Scene Designer*

A Stage setting has no life of its own. Its emphasis is directed toward the performers. In the absence of the actor it does not exist.

The reason we have had realistic stage "sets" for so long is that few of the dramas of our time have been vital enough to be able to dispense with them.

Robert Edmond Jones (distinguished American scene designer and stage director)

DURING THE SECOND and third decades of the present century there was a kind of rule dealing with multiscene musical shows. While the technique evolved *because* of the need to change scenery and keep the show moving at the same time, it affected the libretto. This need to keep going while chang-

---

*Unless otherwise noted, the quotations in this chapter are excerpted from a number of taped interviews I had with the people named.

ing sets was accomplished physically by the use of a *traveler curtain.* This type of curtain moved from side to side. Most often it was made in two equal parts that came together from the two sides of the stage. Sometimes it was a single unit that covered the entire stage front, moving across from one side only, and usually being opened again in the same direction.

These travelers almost invariably had scenes or suggestions of scenes painted on them. That scene might be a park, a street, the facade of a house, or anything desired. It was brightly colored, realistic, but more or less sketchy in style.

These curtains mostly hung in "one" (i.e., on the first pipe, the one farthest downstage, thereby demarcating the acting area nearest the audience) and allowed enough stage space on the audience's side for actors to walk, sing, speak, or parade. Behind the closed curtain, there was an almost complete stage space that could be used for "striking" (removing from the stage) one set and erecting another.

The orchestra usually played lively music during the coming on and taking off of the curtain. The music was a noisy reprise of a song already heard, played in fast tempo and fading out as the curtain concluded its travel in either direction.

The material performed in front of the curtain was occasionally essential to the plot, but more often it was a reprise of the song that had just been sung, or a conversation between two or three people as they moved across the stage, indicating that they had just come from the preceding scene or were on their way to some other specific place. There was no end to the kind of material employed. Whatever it was, there was no secret that this "cross" was an attempt at concealing the scene change (which usually announced itself anyhow with the noise being made backstage!).

These travelers were not always confined to "one." Sometimes they were set further back—in "two" or "three"—always with sufficient space behind them to effect whatever change was needed. There were usually two reasons for the added front space: there was to be a dance—solo or group—framed by a traveler with a different painted background, and the curtained space behind it was planned to be adequate to set the stage for the ensuing scene.

This style of musical production was almost inevitable for

shows, especially in the thirties and forties, when musicals required more scenery. Prior to that time, shows were generally in three acts with one set per act. Since the scenery was usually changed during intermissions, little effort was made to entertain the audience during the changes.

Today, in producing multiscene shows from that era, it is wise to employ the traveler-production technique.

In the shows of the sixties and following, the traveler disappeared in favor of a single basic set—often an abstract background—with set-in pieces that slid on stage from either side, leaving a couple of chairs and a small table, or whatever minimal furniture was needed for suggesting a specific room or locale. The fact that audiences accepted this without fuss was a healthy sign for the theater: it proved that the minds of the beholders could imagine all kinds of things without having them spelled out. With realistic scenery, an audience sees *only* what is given it. Its imagination plays no part. When the scene is merely *suggested*, the audience becomes individually creative.

This simplifying of scenery has produced artistic results. Designer Howard Bay says, "When you are faced with a space, time or financial limitation, this leads you to do the creative process in quite an unusual way that you might not have thought of if all these elements were limitless."

*   *   *

All of the designers I have worked with feel that their initial concept comes from reading the script and hearing the score. Then they have meetings with the stage director to ascertain whether or not he has a special production concept, and, if so, they will be guided by that.

Today's designers have access to all kinds of research material relating to the locale and time period of the play. All of them agree that they do indeed scrutinize the available material, but they do not copy what they see. As designers are creative artists, they digest the drawings and photographs, and their designs represent the places named, but, more important, the places are now presented as seen through their own eyes.

It is best that this question of concept be clearly under-

77

stood at the outset since a failure at communication can lead to endless turmoil, and so much collaboration is required in the production of a musical that turmoil is more the "order of the day" than something unexpected and unusual. So no additional turmoil is wanted.

Collaboration among scene, costume, and lighting designers is essential; like all other artistic matters, there are principles but no rules. Many scene designers look to the costume designers (surprisingly) for their color palettes. When the latter have made decisions based on the needs of the show, fabrics and colors available, the period and locale, they try to create a basic color scheme. With this in mind, the scene designer proceeds to make sketches that would properly complement the projected costumes.

This procedure is, of course, not the only one. Some scene designers prefer to do it in reverse manner—designing scenery, then conferring with the costume designer as to what direction the costume designer may go in regarding color.

Having established their plans and settled the matters of color, the scene and costume designers meet with the lighting designer to ascertain what the latter can conceive that would help achieve the desired overall effects.

How these three work together is a concern of paramount importance. If the kind or color of costumes is wrong for certain scenery, their juxtaposition will be disastrous for both. To complicate matters further, undesirable lighting can change radically all of the real colors, and can fail to provide proper illumination for figures moving in costumes and for the speaking/singing faces.

Collaboration among the three designers has to do with an understanding of the style of the show; the period; and especially whether a scene is to represent day or night, whether the mood is happy or sad, and how these three crafts are expected to complement one another.

One sad example of not considering these aspects carefully is what happens to the Metropolitan Opera production of Mozart's *The Magic Flute*. The great Marc Chagall designed a number of backdrops that, in themselves, are incredibly beautiful. They are literally crowded with multicolored flowers. The singers must live, move, and sing glorious music in front of these drops. However, when one views this production, one can only dream that the singers will somehow fade away because they prevent a full view of the drops!

When lighting is added to this grand melée, things can grow only worse. The lighting designer cannot conceivably locate a focus or a color. Everything is wrong. Thus, it can be seen that a great painter working alone in his studio is no match for the collaboration required in the musical theater. Since *The Magic Flute* has the air of an old fairy tale and requires brilliantly colored and stylized costumes, it should have been clear that scenery should have been as "unbusy" and plain as possible. Every thinking well-dressed lady knows that if she wears a multicolored dress, she will decorate it or herself as sparsely as possible with baubles and other unessential trimmings.

Oliver Smith, designer of many ballets and shows, including *My Fair Lady, Candide, The Sound of Music, Gentlemen Prefer Blondes,* and many others, says:

> The conflict that occurs during collaboration is often very constructive because it opens up all sorts of creative avenues for everyone. There is no successful play or musical that isn't successful because of collaboration. There is no such thing as a show being created by one person.

Scene designer Robin Wagner, in endorsing the practicality of the nonrealistic unit set, has said: "The blocking [placing and moving of the actors] will describe the area of the room—its limits. Writers depend too much on . . . the scenery to provide things which they could do in a line."

I must concur with Wagner in regard to blocking describing the limits of a space without the aid of scenery. I have observed this use of suggestion at work for a long time. John Dexter, the brilliant English director, staged Peter Shaffer's play *The Royal Hunt of the Sun.* At one point a narrator at downstage stage left was commenting on action that was taking place upstage center. Pizzaro's soldiers were holding one another's hands as they carefully rounded a mountain ledge thousands of feet high in the Andes. It was very cold and the wild birds screamed. The path was narrow and icy.

What we actually saw, darkly lit, was a group of soldiers

holding hands, very carefully stepping along, inch by inch, as they disappeared around what might have actually been a dark screen! But we, the audience, were breathless with fear. The blocking accentuated and the actors illustrated what the narrator told, and we believed in the height, the wind and the cold, the narrowness of the path, the iciness. It was all there in our minds' eyes.

The use of a narrator was Shaffer's device, but the same effect could have been achieved by the use of sparse dialogue combined with that slow, danger-filled trodding, close to the backing and around its corner. This is the stuff of theater. It could not be staged this way for film, where the nature of the artifice would be all too apparent. For this sort of epic adventure, film treatment is, in the end, less theatrical.

A Chorus Line (Wagner) used a bare stage with a cyclorama far upstage, each two-foot-wide section of which could be mechanically revolved to form a cyclorama of mirrors. Again, lights played an indispensable part.

Oliver Smith's scenery for *West Side Story* was so designed that one scene dissolved into another. For example, at the end of the scene in the gym, Tony is left alone (the other characters having receded into darkness) and he begins singing "Maria." During the last phrase, the lights, which had previously dimmed to a single spot on Tony, come up to reveal an outdoor night setting, with Tony now standing before a row of tenements, in one of which Maria lives. All scene changes were accomplished in a similar fashion.

In *all* theater—musical and nonmusical—things have apparently become increasingly simple. While this is undoubtedly due in part to increased costs of production, it seems to have begun a trend toward simplicity that is refreshing and in many ways involves the audience to a greater degree, since they are called upon to exercise their imagination.

Of all of the *big* scenic shows to date that *did* work, the ample *Sweeney Todd* (designed by Eugene Lee) makes more and more sense. It was unique in almost every way. Scenically, there was a large false proscenium, its two sides rising to meet at the very top of the stage. It was made of squares of what appeared to be colored glass. There was a background of machinery that was employed only once. Two steel balconies framed each side of the forestage. Most of the action took place stage-center in, around, and above a revolving box-like structure, the lower half of which showed various parts of a pastry shop, while the sideless second floor was a barber shop. One unusual aspect of the production was an army of costumed stagehands (they seemed to be wearing black smocks) who wheeled around several sets of steps of varying heights and placed them (with split-second timing) wherever anyone was descending or ascending, then removed them to less conspicuous places.

This stunning production (directed by Harold Prince) for *Sweeney Todd* was a dark spectacle complementing Sondheim's score, which—strange to say (and, in my opinion, the only way it could have gone)—was mostly amusing and charming, sung against a forbidding background, the production and the music/lyrics enhancing one another.

As noted, nearly all of the action took place in spotlights at the very center of the stage. (Some small scenes took place briefly on stage-right and stage-left). The two principal characters seldom left stage-center.

This almost invariable use of stage-center inspired much discussion as to how effective and how much less expensive the production might have been without the surrounding levels. And, because of the enormous size of the theater and the set, there was a large singing ensemble, an army of electricians operating spotlights on both sides of the stage on each of the three levels, and the aforementioned black-clad stagehands maneuvering sets of rolling stairs.

In a smaller production, the singers, electricians, and stagehands would have been fewer; had it taken place in a much smaller theater, who could say that it might not have been as effective?

*   *   *

It occurs to me that creative people—especially those working in the theater—should always examine their material before they work in a direction opposite to the obvious one.

81

Let me create some examples.

A royal ballroom is, by now, a magnificent cliché. Close your eyes and you see again what you have seen so many times before: a grand crystal chandelier, small gold chairs, a highly polished floor, bright lights, side candelabra, and so on.

Now think for a moment of a somewhat different scenario. You have a two-dimensional cut-out chandelier, amusingly designed and really like nothing ever seen in any known palace. Spaced across the back of the stage you have two men dressed as lackeys with powdered wigs, but wearing blue jeans. Each holds a candelabrum of as few or as many candles as desired. A gold or yellow cyclorama is at the back. The female dancers at the ball wear the *outlines* of hooped skirts that have not been covered with fabric. These can be designed to show their bodies in a lovely way, or grotesquely, or comically. The men wearing tailcoats of various colors, but without shirts and with ordinary trousers—no cliché this, but fresh and perhaps amusing. A seventeenth- or eighteenth-century grand ballroom seen today in a strictly representational way is not new, fresh, *or* amusing.

Or take the park in *Carousel* where Billy Bigelow has his meeting with Julie and Carrie in scene 1. That park could have a new look. Why could it not, for a background, have two long pieces of brown wrapping paper on each of which was freely sketched a green tree—the papers a few feet apart and held up by a ladder (observable by the audience)? A tin pie pan could be suspended to represent the moon. Any bench in the mid-foreground could complete the set if it were properly lit—magically, lightly lit—and so on: created, not copied, even outrageous, but alive.

Whether they are conserving money by going the simple route, or dispensing it lavishly, scene designers are currently in a period of creativity whose richness and disparity has never before existed. Robin Wagner states an important point of view:

> If there is extraneous scenery on the stage, it is a distraction, not a help. If you can eliminate it and start with the premise that nothing is there until it demands to be there, then the space is

82

used in a more theatrical, a more precise way. It must have a "reason."

Robert Edmond Jones was one of America's greatest designers. He was always against the use of real material on the stage and greatly advocated the principle that today's designers are still carrying out. Thirty-seven years ago in his marvelous book *The Dramatic Imagination,* Jones wrote:

> There is no more reason for a room on a stage to be a reproduction of an actual room than for an actor who plays the part of Napoleon to be Napoleon or for an actor who plays Death in the old morality play to be dead.

There is a tale concerning a nonmusical that illustrates what can happen when there is, for any reason, insistence on reality.

The late Jo Mielziner related a horrifying incident relevant to Jones' axiom that occurred in the production of *Tobacco Road* in 1933.

> The action at one point called for an actor to till some dirt with a hoe. The management was advised to put in artificial earth, but they balked at paying for something they could get for nothing more than a nominal hauling fee from a nearby park. After a year on the stage, the real soil, nurtured by generous waterings to keep the dust down and by the heat of the stage lights, had sprouted a most odious and odorous assemblage of weeds and other vegetation, bone white in color, weird in shape, stunted in growth. The insects, and finally, the rodents followed. After a long series of complaints from the employees of the theater and a warning from the Health Department, the management was forced to remove the earth, only to discover that it had also rotted the floorboards of the stage.

*   *   *

The "realization" of scenery, what it becomes when it has been *created,* lit, and set on the stage, has everything to do with the designer's imagination and his true relationship to the book, music, and director. The actual carpentry and painting and the application of the great amount of hardware that allows it to stand, move, be taken away easily, and *"stacked"*—

these and many other practical elements that play necessary parts in this realization—are to be learned more explicitly through observation of practiced craftsmen than by reading any set of instructions.

These physical aspects—building and painting—are necessary, but they are the execution of creative imagination, the basic element without which all the carpentry and the reproduction of design on canvas would fail to exist. The builders and painters are the "middle men" between the scenic artist and the completed stage production.

If I have one specific notion to add—and I have mentioned it earlier—it is the advice, especially to new and as yet nonprofessional designers, to look first for ideas in a direction opposite to the obvious one. This is especially important when the designer is working with material that has been previously designed, photographed, reproduced, and so on. None of us wants to live by copying. Besides, the original musical production on Broadway was extremely expensive, probably elaborate. Why not search for the underlying concept, not the dressing that often conceals it? One potted bush on a stage, surrounded by a blue cyclorama and lit for night, can be almost anything the designer opts it to be. Add one white column and a bench and it becomes a place for lovers to meet. It will function for *any* show provided it is consistent in style with the other scenes in the same show, in this case provided all of the other scenes are equally sparse, that is, indicated, but not spelled out or cluttered.

*   *   *

I have not attempted to describe the methods of making and painting scenery. What we are concerned with here is the *artistry,* the creativity of scene designers, and I thought the best way to be helpful was to quote some thoughts and experiences of the contemporary "greats." Nobody can possibly teach anyone *everything* he needs to know, partly because no person knows everything. However, for a nonprofessional to be stirred and made to begin thinking is indeed the beginning of learning—only the beginning.

Chapter 8

Costume Designer *

THIS SECTION IS ADDRESSED to costume designers, not to those patient ones who execute the designs, or to those others who—more or less silently—take care of keeping the wardrobe clean and in a generally fresh condition.

Within the nonprofessional theater, the methods of making clothes and of handling them backstage before and after performances differ greatly. To begin with, collaboration is an enormous necessity. First, the scene and costume designers must know in detail what each wants to do, and, when they have agreed on color, style, and relationship, they need to have considerable discussion with the lighting designer.

Before these meetings take place, all of them will have read the book of the show, listened to the music, and had in-depth meetings with the stage director, who may have a very

*The quotations in this chapter are excerpted from a number of taped interviews I had with the people named.

specific concept as to the style of the show and how he wishes it to be arrived at in these three visual departments.

Failing to follow this procedure can spell disaster for all three designers as well as for the production itself.

Color is the first thing to be discussed. A production does not have to be monochromatic, but whatever colors and combinations of colors predominate in a set, they must not in any way clash with the costumes. In the same way, a "busy" set would cry out for simple costumes, and a plainer one—a cyclorama, for instance—could accommodate much greater detail in the costumes.

Make-up is another consideration. Sir John Gielgud told me with great disdain of a production of *Othello* in which he starred at Stratford-on-Avon. He was appalled to discover that the basic background was *black,* since this meant that Sir John's face—made swarthy for his portrayal of the Moor—would melt into the background and little of him would be seen except his eyes and his open mouth!

Then there is the matter of collaboration with the lighting designer. Without constant, and complete, communication, there is invariably disaster. There is the story of one costume designer who created a beautiful yellow frock with white collar and cuffs for a young actress. Designer, actress, and director were delighted with it. What the designer did not know was that the dress was to be worn in an exterior night scene when the lights would bathe everything in blue. When this happened, the costume became a most unattractive shade of brown! The lighting *had* to represent night, and so the costume had to be rethought and remade.

There is always the question of style, which must be agreed on carefully even before any of the designers begins to do a sketch. Sometimes this is a general license to let imagination soar, as in a Bosch painting. More frequently the director has an overall concept about a special treatment he plans for the show, and this will dictate the nature of the costumes. Orson Welles did a *Julius Caesar* in the thirties (mentioned previously), during the rise in fascism. In order to relate this play to the audience of that time, he used no togas. Instead, the men looked like gangsters in their long overcoats and wide-brimmed felt hats.

The question of period is always a vital one. Patricia Zipprodt, designer of *Pippin, Chicago,* and many other shows, was involved in a Metropolitan Opera revival of *Tannhäuser.* She held a conversation with the German stage director. In trying to explain what he wanted, he said he wanted the effect of the "thirteenth century as seen through the eyes of the nineteenth-century Baroque!"

Miss Zipprodt interpreted this as follows: "The thirteenth century consists of statues, manuscripts and stained glass windows—and we combine that with a sense of the mid-Victorian at the time when Wagner wrote *Tannhäuser.* Then you marry that with the extreme simplicity of thirteenth-century dress—the simplest period in history." The director's single sentence, based on thought and research, gave the costume designer a clear picture of where she was to go for her basic concept, yet allowed her a wide latitude within which to add her own talents and decisions.

The nonprofessional costume designer will not want to copy the designs made for the original Broadway production. The temptation will always be there since, today, there are so many photographs of scenes and actors appearing in hit shows. However, the entire style of production locally might be so different from the original in concept that costumes similar to those originally designed should not even be a possibility.

*　　　*　　　*

I would like to issue a warning about doing clothes for a period show. Everyone approaching this assignment does research in all kinds of books, books that have become available generally during the past 30 or 40 years.

I have heard from nearly every experienced designer that, after researching the period, they abandon the factual aspects and try to create clothes that serve the central concept of the show and at the same time express their own style.

For decades I have preached this point of view to composers, and it applies to all *creative* people in the theater. It is unnecessary for an American composer—born and bred here—to attempt to write Spanish music just because the show's locale is Spain. What he will wind up with will be *ersatz* Spanish. Until fairly recently, self-respecting artists have not even thought of such a thing. Neither Mozart nor Rossini, writing operas based on French plays set in Seville in 1600, wrote anything remotely Spanish in *The Marriage of Figaro* and *The Barber of Seville,* respectively. At a much later time, Alban Berg composed the music for *Wozzeck*—but *not* music of 1812. Audiences listen to the *style* of the music and, if it seems appropriate, they accept it without consciously weighing it.

In his choice of language, T.S. Eliot putting words into the mouth of Thomas à Becket did not resort to the cliché of imitating middle English. Instead, Eliot wrote as Eliot would have written anything: using contemporary language in Eliot's own style.

The same holds true for visual arts. All of his life, Picasso was inescapably Spanish. Robert Edmond Jones was certainly not Danish in his designs for *Hamlet.*

The costume designer approaching a Civil War play may decide to be authentic and dress the women in hoop skirts, but, beyond that nod to authenticity, the *feeling* of the costumes should represent the designer and the world of *today,* employing patterns and colors that might not have existed at the period of the play. Miles White, who created the costumes for *Oklahoma!, Bloomer Girl,* and many other shows, advises:

> You make them as they were made in their own times. (This has nothing to do with designing.) The corset underneath helps to give the correct posture. When hoop skirts are properly made, the performer can walk through a doorway or sit and they will collapse. Frequently today, the hair-styles worn with such costumes are contemporary, and the dress and the hair unfortunately fail to complement one another.

Theoni Aldredge, who dressed *A Chorus Line,* feels:

> Any period show has to be played for contemporary audiences, so you almost have to look at it through the audience's eyes—

what people *think* 16th Century was—and also we are dealing with a body that is not of the 16th Century—with a contemporary body—most of the time undisciplined. A person in tights doesn't sit the way a person in blue jeans sits.

The costumer must bear in mind the fact that designing clothes for a musical will be influenced tremendously by choreography. Actually, this is also true of the scene designer and especially the lighting designer. The clothes must of course look well, but they must give the dancers the freedom that the choreography demands. The scenery must allow enough space and the lighting must illumine without creating shadows in the wrong places.

Costume designers' difficulties with dancers and their choreographers are legion. Designs are made and approved, but, when the designer is called in to watch a dance rehearsal, he may see that the costumes as approved will not possibly work with the choreography, and changes will have to be made. In one show dancers were to wear armor, which is, of course, unbendable. The designer, after seeing a run-through of the dance in which armor was to be used, had to invent new combinations of materials and reinforcements that would allow the body-bends and still appear to be armor when the bodies stood upright.

Since the nonprofessional designer should avoid copying, he should be on guard against accepting literally the descriptions printed in the published editions of shows. (The same principle applies to the stage director and scenic designer.) Most of the time, these descriptions were the author's ringside view of the finished first production or his idealized view of the show's visual aspects at the time he wrote the play. Even in the original Broadway production of a play or musical, the author's original descriptions of characters are not always carried out.

A case in point concerns the original production of a monumental nonmusical, Tennessee Williams' *A Streetcar Named Desire*.

Lucinda Ballard—a southern lady—was offered the position of costume designer. In talking to the director Elia Kazan, she raised all kinds of objections. Miss Ballard disapproved of Williams' first description of Blanche DuBois in the script. According to Miss Ballard:

> Her first costume, which sets the whole feeling of the character, describes her as wearing a white linen suit and a big hat. In the first place, a white linen suit is a crisp, tailored looking thing, and a big straw hat just isn't Blanche to me. It is supposed to be dusk, and she is terrified and fluttering around like a sick moth: that's what she ought to look like. And I think she ought to have thin blond hair, the kind that is really ash-blond baby hair, and that's why she washes it all the time, and touches it up—and I think she ought to wear pastel colors, and lots of little bows. I think Blanche ought to have a terrible kind of little daintiness.

Miss Ballard's last phrase won over both author and director and she designed the costumes as she had envisioned them.

The majority of printed stage directions are copies of the work achieved by famous directors. These really should not apply to any other production of the same show, because they evolved in working with particular actors, singly and in groups, with specific scenery on a specific stage, probably of a different size from the stage on which the play will next be mounted. When the next director has to work with different actors, he should feel free of these printed "instructions" so that he can put the best show possible on his own stage and his own sets, taking into account all kinds of limitations! These "directions" are not sacrosanct, even if the lines and situations of the show itself are.

Another consideration that the costume designer should bear in mind is "creature comfort." Theoni Aldredge speaks of this very matter: "That performer is going to have to walk, sit, act, and dance, and so I think about comfort.

An inspired designer of scenery or costumes should take advantage, when it is possible to do so, of what is referred to as "the moment." (An example, scenically, might be having many crystal chandeliers suddenly lowered into position from the flies.) In costuming, Irene Sharaff, who designed the clothes for many shows and films (*West Side Story* and *The King and I* are two), created a ballgown for Gertrude Lawrence in *The King and I*. It was Sharaff's feeling (and that of others connected with the production) that the dress—as it swung around in the "Shall We Dance" number—became a third dimension in the duet. It was an unforgettable experience, the result of the costume design and the choreographer's use of the dress.

It is my profound hope that one particular costume difficulty on Broadway is nonexistent in the nonprofessional theater: the stars or leading players can often make a great deal of trouble for the designer. They object to wearing a certain color, or feel that the cut of a collar or neck of a dress is unbecoming. As the star must be placated in the interest of peace, the designer has to redo a great deal of what has already been okayed by the director. The designers can do little to avoid this. In the nonprofessional theater, where there are no stars, it is *hoped* that no one encounters this particular difficulty. If it does occasionally pop up, the designer ought to remind the performer that the image one sees in a mirror one or two feet away is quite different from that on the stage viewed at a distance of from ten feet to perhaps one hundred and fifty. The costume is to delineate the traits and decisions of the *character*, not the actor. In addition, the performer will be lit and made up, and the hair will be appropriate to the role as well as to the performer.

(Some nonprofessional [and even professional] theaters rent their clothes from Eaves-Brooks Costume Co., 21-07 41 Ave., Long Island City, NY 11101. They have an enormous collection of costumes, many of them made for the original productions, and they know precisely what is needed for each character in every previously produced show. These clothes were expensively created, are kept in perfect shape, and are clean. The group desirous of using their services has only to fill out forms as to each person's measurements. Other costume rental companies in other parts of the country provide similar services.)

I should like to quote from the great Robert Edmond Jones in speaking of costumes in John Milton's day: "Documents will not help us here, or at most they will serve only as a starting point from which to proceed. What we are after at this moment is not erudition but evocation."

This sums up the difference between the library and the stage.

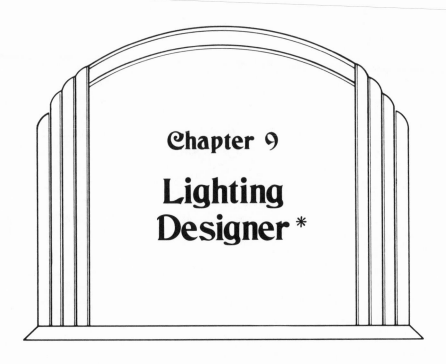

Chapter 9

Lighting
Designer *

"WHATEVER YOU DO, everything still should go back to the show, the story, the music! What does it sound like, what is it about, therefore, what kinds of lights should it demand?"

This statement was made by Jules Fisher, noted lighting designer, whose credentials include the design of lights for *Hair, Butterflies Are Free,* and *You're A Good Man, Charlie Brown.*

This chapter, which deals with the problems of the lighting designer, contains a great deal of advice pertinent to all theater lighting. All of the people quoted are leaders in their field, have learned their crafts as apprentices to leading designers, and are more experienced than most others in their field today.

First, let us consider briefly the place and origin of the

*The quotations in this chapter are excerpted from a number of taped interviews I had with the people named.

lighting designer. Every technical facet of the theater has become more and more specialized. Once, scene designers also designed costumes. Sometimes they lit the show, or perhaps the stage director lit it. Today, because time has become increasingly limited and expensive, and each phase of the operation has become highly sophisticated, it is generally impossible for any one person to perform more than one function.

The lighting designer has grown in importance within the last two decades. With the simplification and reduction of scenery, lighting has been required to add variety to the stage, to delineate small playing areas, to create mood, to define day and night; in musical shows it is often used in special ways to isolate singers or to separate them, one from another, when such an effect is desirable.

A unique difficulty in dealing with lights is stated by Ken Billington:

> Scenery can be photographed, an artist can paint pictures, costumes can be photographed, music can be recorded, words can be written down, but there is no way to record lighting. Lighting is a totally visual art that you experience as it is happening.
>
> Scenery and costumes and even performers do not exist without lights, and the lighting designer has the responsibility to bring all of these elements to life through application of his knowledge, taste and skill.

Jules Fisher elaborates on the illusory nature of light itself that further explains Billington.

> You don't see light, you see its effects. You see it bouncing off this piece of paper, but the light is actually between the light bulb and here. You don't see it until something captures and reflects it: it has to hit something . . . my work only looks as good as what it is going to land on, so if I design a great pool of red light and it is going to land on something green, it is not going to look good.

The proper handling of lights in a musical show requires certain special considerations, and most designers (scene, lighting, and costume) agree that they are influenced strongly by the music. Fisher continues, "Since music is the core of musicals, it will suggest how the show should be lit. Is it a musical that should be lit with a lot of backlight; should people sparkle and stand forward? I think some musicals, yes, but others, no."

According to John Gleason, one of the hardest things in doing a musical is the fact that, like the set and costume designers, he has to work in advance of rehearsals. "And some of the most important work done on a musical takes place in the rehearsal hall, so that certain instincts have to start taking place for us when we hear the music played on the piano, and the orchestration can settle the matter of color for me."

Fisher says that the relationship of light with music is "crucial." "If a scene ends with music, what does the music do? I think the lighting designer must listen and in some way complement it. This doesn't mean he must *follow* the music (if it fades, the light must also fade), but that lights must complement music."

As an example, at the end of the bench scene in *Carousel* the music builds to a climax, an essential one. Inasmuch as the climax ends the scene, the lights should probably *fade* parallel with the musical crescendo and then black out at the very end.

It is generally estimated that the lighting of a musical for the first time requires about 15 hours. However, the designer must have organized his work in advance and have done his "homework" or there will be bedlam, and the hours needed to accomplish his work will be multiplied.

The reader should be reminded that each light cue is attached to a specific word, move, note of music, entrance, exit, or anything else that the lighting designer feels begins to motivate a light change. The cue may bring about a sudden effect, such as lightning, or a power failure, for example, or it may be the start of a long effect, such as a sunrise or sunset that can occupy ten or fifteen minutes or longer. The point is that it must have a definite place for starting and that place must be attached to a specific event that is clear-cut and will never vary from one rehearsal or performance to the next.

The eyes of the audience must be directed by the use of lights and, sometimes, scenery as to just where they must look.

The late, great scene designer, Jo Mielziner, painted his sets darker at the top so that the eyes would look at the bottom, where they should, in order to see the people. Fisher remarks that "People are only six feet high, and they don't get bigger at the top. And with a set that is painted light at the top, your eye is going up to the top, because the lights are all mounted at the top."

Tharon Musser has this to say: "One of our main jobs as lighting designer is not only to support the mood or the feeling of the scene, but to tell the audience where to look. You don't distract them with a hot spot 'up right' when you have something important happening 'down left.' You balance it. And the audience pulls their eye where you want it."

Fisher makes an interesting point when he says that directors—unable to articulate what satisfies them—will ask for more light on a particular character. "There is plenty of light on the stage. The dissatisfaction may be due to where the light is coming from, what color it is, or where else it is falling. Maybe it is falling on a lot of distracting elements: the answer, very often, to not being able to see a performer, is to *take away* some of the light from somewhere else."

In lighting musical shows, one of the greatest difficulties is in lighting dancers. To do the best possible job, the lighting designer needs to study the movement from three points of view. First, the overall movement: *where* do the dancers move? Second, is there small important movement with their feet or their hands? Third, what is the mood and feeling of the particular dance?

All of this is complex beyond anyone's imagination because you are dealing not only with light but with the greater problem, shadows. Fisher has much to say about this:

> A lot of people criticize me for using too much equipment. I need a lot of equipment sometimes, not necessarily to make it bright, and I don't use all of the instruments at the same time: I use the equipment in different scenes, I use it in different ways. I use one set of lights for one mood and another set for another, and I may use some lights for just a ballet. They may never be used again during the evening. I think you have a two-hour period to create a memorable event in the audience's mind.

In a musical, sometimes, in order to get the intensity you need, you put up many, many lights: lights in the balcony, lights in the box-booms, lights on pipes over the stage, and from the wings. If you light a scene with lights from all these sources, eight or nine, you are going to have eight or nine shadows, and shadows will make fine movement confusing. So lighting a Bob Fosse show versus a show with another choreographer, I might use fewer instruments of a higher power in the wings. In most musicals, I would use four lamps in "one" going across the stage from left to right from the first boom to provide a color wash. With Bob Fosse's shows, I do everything with three rather than four, because I want to have less shadow in order for you to see this articulate movement. Here is an example that, as a lighting designer, I would do something special for that particular director-choreographer.

Tharon Musser says, "In a musical you need to give yourself as much variety of angles as possible because you are not really concerned with faces but with 'making sculpture'—concerned with the body movement. For the book-points of a musical, you are concerned with the faces."

In the nonprofessional theater, many of the principles illustrated in Fisher's and Musser's accounts may seldom apply, since most theaters cannot afford such elaborate equipment—all set to specification of the designer. When this is true, I believe it is largely necessary to resort to the use of one or more spotlights—"follow-spots"—that can be used to "pursue" the moving figures wherever they are on the stage. While this is far from ideal, it is a practical solution to an otherwise impossible situation.

If the spotlight is to be employed, dance numbers will appear more advantageously if the choreographer and lighting designer have meetings before the dances are begun and throughout the rehearsal period. The lighting designer will be able to point out specific choreography that will be impossible to light, and in the end the entire production will be better served. In a sense, this kind of collaboration is not far removed from what has to be considered carefully when a choreographer is creating dances for television. In the latter case, it is the camera that dictates some curtailment on the choice between "long shots" and "close-ups," neither of which is ideal in photographing group dancing.

The spotlight is practically the "best friend" of musical theater. Its association with musical shows in America goes back as far as anyone can remember. While musicals were "growing up," the spotlight performed many functions, providing easy solutions to lighting problems that later became clichés when more sophisticated lighting equipment was available. For example, it was customary for at least 40 years to use the spotlight on all solo and duet singers. When love songs were sung, all other stage lighting was dimmed down while the singers were bathed in spotlights employing a variety of different gelatins according to the stage director's wish; afterwards the lighting was restored to "normal." Sometimes the color was amber, or pink, or light blue; later on, white was used. In comedy songs the stage lights were not dimmed, as the theory had always been that comedy must be played in bright light and romance in dim light. In both cases, however, the spotlight was employed.

In the past, stars were always in the spotlight. When one or two people were playing in front of a traveler curtain, spotlights were used to follow them across the stage. The uses of the spotlight should be obvious, but one hopes that no production today is entirely dependent on one. It should be used when needed and especially when more subtle stage lighting is not available. A mixture of both, especially when the brightness of the stage tends to dim the presence of the spotlight, is advisable.

Several things should be remembered. Scenery, costumes, and performers do not exist without lighting. Performers should always take preference over scenery and costumes, although the latter will be clearly featured when the performers who wear them are properly lighted.

It is also important for lighting designers to collaborate. While the script will present some ideas, the music perhaps others, it is the director who should be relied upon to gather all of these up into one single concept that should affect all of the designers at work on one show.

Today, when there is often less scenery than formerly

used, the role of the lighting designer is greater than ever before. Equipment to sustain this demand is available in the
Broadway theater. If it is less accessible in the nonprofessional
theater, the collaboration between scene and lighting designers should be even more intense so that sets will be lit as they
need to be.

I have never believed that more is better. The less money
there is to be spent in theatrical production, the more imagination is required of the various people who conceive the
show. Sets and costumes are expensive. Buying lighting equipment is obviously more expensive at the beginning than renting it. However, with trimmed budgets, the lighting designer
can go a long way to complement and to create what would
otherwise be seen as lacking on the stage.

To make an unlikely example: two spotlights on either side
of the stage, their beams crossing at an angle and off-stage-
center, supplemented by dim lights from booms—all of these
perhaps white—can fill an entire stage with magic. Nothing
else need be used. The balcony scene in *West Side Story* could
be played in such a set-up, even without the "balcony."

But there are unlimited ways in which the judicious and
imaginative use of whatever is available can make anyone forget that anything at all is lacking. It is the employment of such
limited material that tends to create style.

Before ending this chapter, I would like to quote lighting
authorities with regard to several other specific matters.

A rule of thumb: the principle of complement. When the
set is colorful and "busy," and the costumes and movements
frenetic, the lighting design serves best when it is as simple as
possible. The reverse is also true. When the set is very simple,
and even if the costumes are "fussy" in color and design, the
lighting can help to provide a sense of liveliness that could be
wanting.

Fisher is critical of those who do not employ or comprehend the importance of "back lighting."

> Back lighting is usually missing in regional theater—and it's the
> real core of a Broadway musical. People's hair stands up. Re-
> member you are in a theater where there are from 1,100 to
> 1,600 seats in a Broadway theater. Sometimes people are 75 to

100 feet away. In order to see people at that distance, one of the things you do is provide a lot of back lighting, lighting that will hit their shoulders, the back of their hair—and give them definition to stand out from the rest of the set. Most amateur productions, community theater productions, are lit with equipment that exists in the local high school, which may be lights in the front of the balcony, and from the ceiling. They often lack the equipment to light the performers' backs. It is expensive to have as many lights in the back as you do in the front, but that is one of the main differences between Broadway and elsewhere. There is a separation between the performers and the sets.

Here is a different point. There is an ever-increasing movement to do away with the front curtain. To my own way of thinking, this belongs in the same category as eschewing overtures. In both instances, much theatrical excitement is done away with. If you have time to study the scenery from the moment you are seated, the set has no impact when the play begins. Robert Edmond Jones felt that the success of scenery was to be judged only as it served the actors who moved in front of it. In that case, familiarity with scenery prior to the beginning of the show is ill-advised. Personally, I do not like it. Even the physical experience of seeing a curtain rise is always thrilling to me.

The failure to have an overture is something like saying, "Folks! Don't be deceived. This is not a musical show." The overture has always been equated in my mind with a circus parade in a small American town. It is a matchless experience.

In line with the curtainless stage, lighting designers increasingly hang lights in the auditorium itself: above the proscenium, outside the proscenium on the sides, and in the boxes on both sides of the stage. The fact of the lights is in itself not a problem, and many of these locations are not new. What has happened only fairly recently is that the lights are not masked or concealed in any way.

Tharon Musser comments: "If you decide that all the lamps are going to show, and you aren't going to have masking, it should be based on a unique concept as to how the show is going to be presented, and not just because it is easy or because somebody just got a whim one day and decided to do it that way."

So much for setting a style and remaining consistent with it.

Much fault (justifiably) is found with directors and choreographers who are unable to read plans, designs, and models of sets, because they are responsible for a great deal of trouble for themselves. Too often they are surprised by the height of steps after they have been built and positioned on the stage. Or they have not bothered to remember that a light boom has been placed at a certain point where they plan to dance or to place a performer.

Fisher raises an interesting point that opens an entirely different vista: "How do we focus attention? What is the last image that you want the audience to see? Do you want it to be his face or her face or both faces? Or none? Do you want to see them in silhouette, and to see the sky last? The possibilities are great. The lighting designer has to pick the right one for the right moment."

The ideas implicit in this brief statement do indeed open up many other questions about lighting. They point to the detail rather than the overall view, and, if the new lighting designer will give himself to finding the answers, he will discover many other facets of his craft that were formerly hidden to him.

Learning the art of lighting has always been an apprenticeship process. Billington remembers:

> Jean Rosenthal passed what she knew on to Tharon Musser who passed it on to me. I have passed it on to my assistants. We have refined and put our own things with it. But we are craftsmen in what we do. And it is very strange to know that no matter what we do, we can only remember it.
>
> Apprenticeship is the only way to learn what theater is about, how to deal with crazy directors and idiot stage managers and geniuses and how it all happens. And when they don't laugh at the jokes it is always because the lights aren't bright enough and it is not that the jokes aren't funny.

This "accusation" does not fall solely on the lighting designer. When a new song does not work, the fault is first the orchestrator's, then the conductor's. When scenery does not

100

function properly, it is the fault of costumes and then lights. This mêlée is unending.

I would also add a word of comparison between all Broadway lighting equipment and an increasing number of college, regional, and nonprofessional theaters.

Broadway theaters with very few exceptions are old, and they are rented to producers on a "four-wall" basis, which is to say that they contain no equipment. Everything of a mechanical nature needed for a particular show must be rented, especially lights and switchboards. These simply do not exist until the lighting designer of a particular show draws up a plan, and orders and installs what is necessary.

In many new nonprofessional theaters, all necessary equipment has been installed at the outset, or it has been added gradually; in many places there is a plethora of lights that hang permanently as a part of the building and can be rehung and refocused as desired. Most important, the most modern "memory" switchboards are currently too expensive to be bought for a single production, although they are beginning to appear in a number of colleges and regional theaters.

In other words, Broadway producers—with each new show—must pay considerable sums of money for the lighting equipment the designer calls for. This is an investment that recurs with every new show. In the nonprofessional theater, although the equipment may be limited, it is nevertheless omnipresent. This is an advantage, since, if budgets allow additional expenditures for lights, whatever is procured becomes part of an ever-expanding permanent set-up.

Finally, I would like to present a very general and simple lighting program of my own making. As a broad example of the most primitive needs of a show, the solutions to which may have to suffice under some nonprofessional conditions, let us list the scenes in *Carousel* as regards lighting in a general way:

PROLOGUE AND ACT I, Sc. 1: Night—and it is important that this is clear. (Night on the stage is not absence of light, but special light that evokes the *feeling* of night.)

Sc. 2: Out-of-doors and June. (The evocation of seasons requires much help from lights.) This is usually a garden. The use of warm colors in the lights would contribute much.

ACT II, Sc. 1: Night, with spotlights picking out several solo singers from an ensemble.

Sc. 2: Also night, but scene 1 is gay and scene 2, brooding.

Sc. 3: "Up There" is a bright scene in a part of heaven. It is comedic, farcical, and warm. There should be a feeling of space.

Sc. 4: Beach Ballet—colorful and definitely day.

Sc. 5: In front of Julie's cottage—day, but again the mood is brooding, perhaps slightly foggy.

Sc. 6: An outdoor graduation, filled with optimism and brightness. Clean and sharp.

These notes on *Carousel* lighting are very general, but they may illustrate basic requirements minus a thousand subtleties that must be omitted when abundant equipment is not available, or lighting designers are not yet sufficiently experienced with their craft.

Everyone who works on a show must become a part of the entire group that, working together, can help to create something wonderful. It is my belief that, upon seeing a really fine new musical show, you do not leave the theater "whistling" the scenery, the costumes, the lights, or the libretto, but you should have had one single glorious experience to which each of the craft artists contributed important and inseparable elements, making it one grand entity.

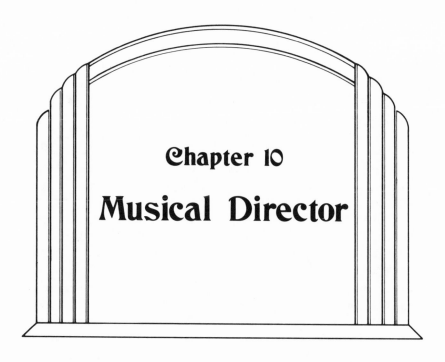

Chapter 10

Musical Director

THE MUSICAL DIRECTOR'S POSITION in the regional theater is somewhat different from that of his Broadway counterpart. He will not be affected by the composer and the latter's wishes. Except in rare cases, he will not be dealing with the requirements of unions, which set wage scales based on hours. He will have seen previous productions or motion pictures of the chosen show (the film will more than likely not have reproduced the original stage version), and he will have the cast record album as a guide in some ways.

At this point I must clarify my position regarding use of the cast album and the cast album itself. Many conductors do not study the recording, whereas many others do. In my opinion, it is a foolish act of egotism or an unnecessary "declaration of independence" not to refer in some respect to the cast album. I feel that this should, for reasons to be mentioned presently, be of some special help. However, the recording should *not* be played until the conductor has already learned the score. In this way, listening to the record will be more meaningful, presenting familiar signposts along the way. Then it will raise some valuable questions in the mind of the conductor: do tempos of this or that differ from the conductor's concept, and, if they do (and they will), which seems more logical and more in the style and spirit of each song? Then, too, the conductor will have the only picture he can have, until he rehearses the orchestra, of what the orchestra will sound like, since he will probably never be furnished an orchestral score. (Orchestral scores are used by the *first* conductor at his first reading in order to *see* the orchestrations and to correct errors. After that, all conductors use the more wieldy "conductor's part," which is a condensation of the very tall four-bars-to-the-page score. Use of the latter at a performance would necessitate perpetual page-turning, sometimes a page every four seconds!) Therefore, if the new conductor listens to the recording he will get a fair idea of the sounds he may expect from his orchestra.

So much for the advisability of listening to the cast album. There are other considerations of which very few people seem aware. The record producer has a point of view that differs greatly in many respects from that of the theater producer. He has to conceive a product that the purchaser will want to hear again and again. His concept will require cutting some songs (reprises, mostly), and cutting all dance music. Some fast songs appear too fast on a record, and some slow songs too slow. In an attempt to avoid both problems, tempos are frequently altered. Sometimes the sequence of the songs in the show is altered on the record, especially when two slow ones appear consecutively. Therefore, all things considered, the cast album may not be an accurate guide, but, once the new conductor has become familiar with the score, can be "interesting" and, in some subtle ways helpful.

A personal anecdote here—since I have conducted so many cast albums—will not be out of place. When I conducted Menotti's opera, *The Consul*, the record producer told Menotti that the opera was too long for the three records (six sides), and he wanted the composer to excise "X" minutes. At the recording studio the producer suggested further cuts, which Menotti refused to make. Instead, Menotti addressed himself to me and asked me to conduct everything faster! Some years later when I listened to the album (I seldom listen to my albums), I was shocked at hearing everything played *too* fast.

The absence of union restrictions will allow more freedom in making schedules, but the musical director in the non-professional theater will encounter other kinds of restrictions that will more than balance those imposed on Broadway.

On the plus side, the size of chorus and orchestra in the nonprofessional theater is unlimited except by stage and orchestra-pit space, availability of certain instruments, and the taste of the musical and stage directors. The number of rehearsals and the length of each will be determined *only* by the amount of time the directors think essential to performing the music properly.

Let me explain each of these items more clearly.

The musical director, with the aid of the local "presenter," must calculate availability of his players, be aware of school demands or working hours that will inevitably interfere, and consider these factors in relation to the difficulties of the orchestra parts of the particular show that is scheduled for performance. Having estimated the necessary rehearsal time, the musical director should order the orchestra parts as far in advance of performances as he deems necessary for accomplishment of his players' tasks. However, it must be understood that early rental will add to the cost.

Apropos of rentals: it often happens that the published vocal score may differ in this or that detail from the rented piano-conductor part, and that discrepancies in the lyrics also occur. The reasons are so numerous that they could fill an entire book, and to no purpose, since they follow no consistent pattern. To list only a few:

The composer prefers an earlier or postproduction version of some musical detail.

The composer has always resented a musical cut and now seizes on this opportunity to restore it.

105

The editor feels that certain lyrics are too risqué (imagine that!). Actually, for example, the correct lyrics of "Bewitched, Bothered and Bewildered" were never published in the sheet music, and they appeared nowhere in print until years after the close of the first production, when the vocal score was finally published.

There are simple human errors.

The moral to this situation, as regards nonprofessional workers who are at the mercy of noncompatible versions, is to be cautious and, when the discrepancies are detected, to choose the version that is preferred and causes the least amount of trouble!

In many nonprofessional places, shows will be performed with one or two pianos. As noted earlier, some rental agencies have two-piano arrangements, or arrangements for band. Perhaps—depending on the style of the show and availability of adequate players—the musical director may decide to do the show with a "combo." Definition of this word is extremely flexible. It may mean piano, bass, and drums; piano, bass, drums, and one saxophone or one trumpet; or any of a number of other combinations.

One facet of the musical director's position should be clarified. The average theatergoer, if he gives a single thought to the man in the pit who "waves the stick," considers him the orchestra leader. Since this is far from a complete explication of his activities, let us define the musical director's duties.

First, he must learn the music. He normally has most to do and most to say at auditions regarding all roles requiring singers, whether principals or ensemble. Knowing the musical score, he advises the producer as to the minimum number of singers he feels are needed. This number is arrived at through examination of the choral sections that are divided into parts (probably soprano, alto, tenor, and bass) and the importance of that particular music to the show. If all ensemble music is written for unison voices (everyone singing the same notes), there is no problem. The chances are excellent that the dancers will be singing at the same time, or that the ensemble will consist only of dancers who can sing. However, at the climaxes of some shows, the vocal parts may be divided into four, five, six, or more parts, which division clearly calls for a greater number of skilled singers.

The vocal chorus will rehearse well before the orchestra, which normally would begin a week (more or less) prior to the first dress rehearsal. The musical director will *teach* the music to the singers and attempt to form an ensemble—a vocal group that sings together. Even after these choruses are learned perfectly, they need frequent review, especially while the singers are being physically moved about the stage by the choreographer or stage director. During this phase they are no longer sitting next to others who sing their same part; as a result, many of them will forget their separate parts and start singing the melody. This unlearning and relearning process is endless. Even in a Broadway show, the ensemble singers need frequent—daily, if possible—review of their choruses.

The musical director, with the invaluable aid of a good pianist, will need time to work with each of the principals separately. This has a twofold purpose. First, the principal will need instruction—daily when possible, after the songs are learned—and, second, these rehearsals tend to establish an invaluable rapport between singer and conductor.

The musical director must also find time to attend some book rehearsals (those held by the stage director) in order to "feel" song cues, to time as accurately as possible the music (underscoring) that is played between parts of a song when the performers are speaking.* Also, by attending as many of these rehearsals as possible, he will gradually develop a sense of the tempo of the show as a whole.

The musical director must also prepare and conduct the orchestra, and let me make it clear at the outset that it is far easier to conduct the Boston Symphony Orchestra than to create an orchestra out of less experienced players! The skill and

---

*The music played under dialogue is often like a parenthesis between two parts of a song. The singer sings, then speaks, then finishes the song. It is absolutely essential that the background music under dialogue be timed out so carefully that the singer is not required to wait for even one second before resuming his song, and the volume of the music held down so the actor need not shout to be heard over the orchestra.

experience of orchestra players, especially where age and consistent playing are limited, may be circumscribed. Such players will be aided considerably by:

1. individual coaching or "woodshedding" when necessary ("woodshedding" is a common term for practicing a part alone and away from the rehearsal)
2. sectional rehearsals
3. schedules spread out over a long period of time.

Some of the players may be inexperienced students who will, at first, not comprehend the style of the music, relationship of the individual to the ensemble as a whole, and the need for submergence as a solo player to sectional participation.

Some of the players may be considered "professionals" in that they are older and more experienced than the younger, newer students. However, in most towns, colleges, and even in cities away from cosmopolitan New York, Los Angeles, and other metropolises, the demand for musicians on a theatrical level has dwindled. Many professional players have thus been forced to earn necessary income from teaching—a situation that at least keeps them in touch with their instrumental technique—or, in too many places, these players earn their livelihoods by working in a variety of unrelated jobs that provide necessary regular income. This situation is certainly regrettable, but without the opportunity to play regularly and earn their livelihoods through playing, these musicians must lose the incentive to keep in practice, and an inevitable "rustiness" will result.

Because of either inexperience or a kind of stagnation, the players may want to read and practice their parts ("woodshed") in advance of or away from ensemble rehearsals. Often this kind of preparation is indispensable. Students will also benefit from occasional supervision provided by the musical director.

Depending upon the difficulty of the music and the extent of inexperience, the musical director may obtain better end results by calling "sectional rehearsals": he will rehearse all of the string players alone, then all of the reeds, then the brass, and so on. It is sometimes beneficial to have one or two members of the rhythm section rehearsing with these sectional players. A guitar, a rhythm drummer (not a xylophone player or a tympanist, who will add color but not rhythm), a string bass player, and/or a pianist will help the musical director to mold his sectional players into the ensemble, and the players in turn will be given a sense of the "feeling" of the music when they are supported by any part of the rhythm section.

When the musical director has had the opportunity to prepare sections, he should try to put together the entire orchestra, a few numbers at a time. Not only will this help him to create the final ensemble, but it will boost the morale of the players considerably. Very often the musical director will feel self-congratulatory when he has succeeded in getting together one particularly difficult number. It will probably have consumed hours of work, and now *it is done!* Or is it? The chances are good that it *is* done at the moment—the culmination of hours of work on this one piece. However, the score of a musical show (including "change" music, overtures, entr'actes, etc.) will number 20 to 30 pieces. It is then advisable to begin each rehearsal with a "review" of two or three already prepared numbers before going ahead to something new. This repetition will not only keep the players familiar with their accomplishment, but it will not allow them to forget, and eventually it will "limber up" their sense of style through familiarity and a lessened concern with individual details such as notes, rests, and so on. Gradually the orchestra will actually "perform" the music.

Recently I had an unusual problem when I was invited to conduct an excellent European orchestra in a program of American music. The program would have caused little difficulty to an American orchestra, but to these European players the style seemed bewildering. I had read through the two most difficult works (they were not inherently difficult but were strange to these otherwise excellent players) at a first rehearsal. It was clear to me that the orchestra had minimal difficulty in playing the notes, but the ensemble effect showed that the players failed to comprehend the style of this music.

At the second rehearsal I had to explain that we were going to play only the first eight bars of one piece, and that I wanted to hear *only* the first flute and first violins (they were playing the same musical line); I begged the others to play softly. Because of this generally correct (if inartistic) balance, the entire orchestra began to hear the "music." I asked to hear the following sixteen bars, with *only* the celli and the bassoons playing loudly, and all other players as accompaniment.

In this way—slowly and painstakingly—the entire piece was gone through. After that we played the entire work from beginning to end, the players observing the dynamics I had asked for. While this run-through was far from "finished," the piece made sense to the players (and to me!) for the first time. Afterwards we were able to work out more subtle dynamics and develop style, because the players themselves were gradually able to comprehend the "sense" of the piece and were then in a position to help me in achieving a proper performance.

No players—experienced or inexperienced—can participate in making a performance if they are not guided by the musical director in understanding the piece they are trying to perform: notes first, balance next, and finally style.

It is customary in all producing situations and on all levels to have what is known as an "Italian" rehearsal, after the orchestra and singers have been separately prepared. At this rehearsal the two elements are coordinated for the first time. It is advisable to hold this rehearsal either in a large rehearsal hall or with everyone—including the orchestra—on stage. There should be no attempt at achieving a balance between instruments and voice. The main purpose of this rehearsal is to have the vocalists *hear* the orchestration, to test their ability to "find the starting notes" that they have found easily when working with a piano. With orchestra, everything will seem different.

Likewise, the dancers will experience a different feeling when they work with the orchestra. Rhythms will be the same ones they have heard at every prior rehearsal, but, because different instruments are now playing the music they have heard only on a piano, they may at first experience some difficulty in "locating" what they depend on musically. In rehearsing a major dance number or ballet with the orchestra for the first time, the piece may have to be repeated several times.

While the musical director should have prepared himself by attending as many dance rehearsals as possible, he will nevertheless not be conducting the orchestra *precisely* as the pianist had taped the same music. There will inevitably be some difference in musicality between the orchestra and the piano. Adjustments will need to be made by both conductor and choreographer.

During the orchestral preparations, installation of the lighting and scenic parts of the production will be proceeding. When these are as nearly finished as they can be—without the performers on stage—the cast will be added and will go through a long technical rehearsal that may have to be extended to several sessions before the show will have been gone through—from beginning to end—one time. In these rehearsals, which are intended to perfect the *technical* aspects of the show, music is of little or no importance, since *performing* the show is also unimportant: one rehearsal pianist will be able to do whatever may be required. It is not essential that the musical director be present. If small changes affecting music are requested, the pianist should be capable of cutting or repeating music necessitated by scenic or costume changes and to convey these variations to the musical director, who will finalize them.

When the technical factors have been accomplished there will be a first dress rehearsal. Sometimes the orchestra will participate, although, if there are to be other dress rehearsals, it may be as well to use only piano again since there will probably be many stops and starts caused by stage matters that have nothing to do with music.

At the first run-through of the show at which the orchestra is employed, much attention should be paid to balancing it with the stage. When the orchestra is too loud, the musical director should be informed *at the time*, although any precise adjustment requires the presence of an audience in the theater since that presence greatly affects the acoustics. (A theater full of people will absorb a good deal of the orchestral sound.)

At these rehearsals, it is often the best procedure *not* to stop the show to fix anything because the cast and the musical director will be unable to arrive at an overall show tempo if there are interruptions. Instead, the stage director, producer, and choreographer should take notes of all faults, and these should be given *after* the run-through (not during the intermission), in this order: notes to the cast as quickly as possible so they can get out of costumes and makeup; then to the stage manager (with regard to lights and scenery) and to the musical director. Each of the latter should be given sufficient time at a rehearsal the following day (not at a run-through) to give individual notes, make changes when changes are desirable, and to *rehearse* these speedily before the next run-through. Too many changes made at a single rehearsal are inadvisable since they tend to confuse everyone.

The musical director may have made notes, if only mental, during the first orchestra dress rehearsal, of things he was able to observe from his vantage point that may not apply to his particular department. He should pass these on to the stage director, stage manager, or choreographer, as they apply.

As in every other aspect of the theater, discipline within the orchestra is of prime importance. The members of the orchestra are required to sit in the pit during long intervals of the show when they are not playing. It is often difficult and boring to sit quietly without talking to fellow musicians or shifting restlessly about. This can distract the audience, and also the performers. In my own experience, I have encouraged the players to bring books to the pit (that is, after the first several performances). I have always frowned on newspapers, since turning pages can be noisy and attention getting.

The musical director is not exempt from applying a sense of discipline to himself. As he sits (between numbers) often higher than the pit (he will need to follow the action and dialogue on the stage and he attracts less attention when he does not suddenly hop up into view), he should sit quietly and make as few movements as possible.

Discipline within the orchestra should also include punctuality (15 to 30 minutes before the call to go into the pit), a pride in warming up their instruments before entering the pit, conscientious tuning, and wearing clothes that have been agreed upon as uniform. A dark jacket and white shirt (black bow-tie for men) are always preferable, especially since the dark jacket will not reflect light. However, for many years now, since the upper half of the player is all that is visible to the audience, many players have scrupulously dressed in the manner described above, but have worn a variety of skirts or trousers and an even wider variety of shoes, including sneakers, golf shoes, boots, or whatever each player chooses. This is acceptable as long as the bottom halves of the players remain out of sight.

The visibility of the theater orchestra is also in a state of flux. *No Strings* was the first show to have its musicians "piped in" from a backstage area, with the musical director watching the stage action on a television monitor. *I Do! I Do!* was played by the orchestra seated at the very back of the stage, partially hidden by a backdrop.

At least at the start of its run, *Jesus Christ, Superstar* put the orchestra back in the pit, but covered over with a black cloth; *A Chorus Line* is played in a covered pit. When these conditions obtain, the dress of the orchestra musicians is of no importance and the men and women wear casual clothes or whatever else they find most comfortable.

Conversely, *Chicago* put its orchestra on top of a platform at stage center, and the dress of these fully visible musicians became the responsibility of the show's costume designer.

*   *   *

Although the stage manager in effect "runs" the show, he is generally powerless, during a performance, to speed up a limp show or to relax one that is overly frenetic. It is the musical director, at the moment when he feels things sliding or racing, who has the power, with the orchestra under his baton, to energize the stage personnel or to pull it back when things seem to be getting out of hand.

Opening nights (first performances) are the times when everyone tends to rush ahead. I recall one opening on Broadway *(Wonderful Town)* when the star, Rosalind Russell, requested that I, the musical director, come to her dressing room at intermission. She was *positive* that the orchestra was playing all of her songs in lower keys! I explained that, be-yond the fact that this was untrue, it would have been impos-sible. Miss Russell's "feeling" was a product of her wanting to go faster and higher because of opening night "nerves." I as-sured her that she was mistaken, that she was doing extremely well, and I left her satisfied and happy!

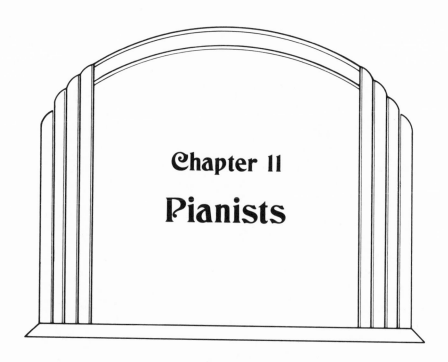

Chapter 11
Pianists

THE REHEARSALS of a musical show are always fraught with difficulties of all kinds. Some of these are indigenous to the nature of any show. Rehearsing a musical show, however, with a pianist who has difficulties with playing the music accurately and fluently can turn an already complex situation into a nightmare.

Many musical directors became musical directors through the excellent work they did in numerous productions as pianists, and then as assistant conductors.

In the school and nonprofessional situation, the musical director may be "number one" pianist at rehearsals, although, if he can avoid taking on this role, he will find vocal ensemble rehearsals easier and better realized. He certainly cannot exist without at least one other skilled person to play piano at rehearsals and finally in the pit.

Although Broadway musicals require the services of three pianists, one of these is given over entirely to the choreographer. This is the dance arranger. He plays all dance rehearsals while composing the music for the ballets.

In the nonprofessional theater the dance music has long ago been set, and is indeed in print in the vocal score. I am advised that in the nonprofessional theater the musical director often conducts the rehearsal pianist in making tape recordings of all dance numbers for the choreographer's use while working out the steps. This happens after the musical director, choreographer, and stage director have gone over the music to determine any desired cuts. If such cuts are made subsequently, a new tape is made.

In my opinion, this method is an exceedingly good one. It saves time for the pianist, and ensures that the tempos remain consistent. The idea of the musical director's conducting the pianist in the making of the tapes is also excellent, since the tempos will be those decided upon by the person who will eventually conduct them.

In the formation of a new show on Broadway, the rehearsal pianist must be:

an expert sight-reader

able to play fluently from lead sheets* with chord symbols

able to transpose *at sight* any music that is written out or exists only as a lead sheet

able to play in a precise and strong rhythmic manner

able to follow the conductor

able to play without visible tensions

In the school or nonprofessional musical theaters, transposition is not necessary as often as on Broadway, especially when the show being rehearsed has been cast so that the sing-

---

*"Lead sheets" consist only of melody lines, often with chord symbols that indicate the harmony.

ers can negotiate the range of the printed music. Lead sheets are seldom used in revivals. But sight-reading, rhythmic precision, and ability to follow the conductor are all essential qualities.

The business of "visible tension" should be briefly discussed. Too many excellent pianists play and "read" music well—but with an obvious display of nervousness. Since this is both contagious and irritating, it is a situation that ought to be avoided.

The pianist ought to be so interested in the progress of rehearsals that he knows, listens, hears, and reacts to whatever is happening. If the conductor stops in the middle of a bar to make a correction, he will say where he wants to resume. Too frequently, the pianist is the very last person to understand where that is!

If the pianist has a good ear, it is more than likely that he will hear small but important details relating to an "inner" part—an alto or tenor—who is persistently singing an incorrect note or rhythm. If he becomes aware of these kinds of deviations, he should choose an unobtrusive moment at rehearsal to tell the conductor.

I have been asked two questions that I cannot possibly answer, and it seems dubious to me that they are answerable! The first is, "Where can good rehearsal pianists be found?" This is analogous to, "Where is the end of the rainbow?" The answer can only be, "Anywhere." Good rehearsal pianists *can* be found. I have usually been blessed, and *all* of my pianists have eventually become conductors.

Apropos of the question, I was conducting a series of four musical shows at a festival in San Juan, Puerto Rico. When we came to *West Side Story*, I realized with alarm that no average pianist could play that music, especially the dance music. Suddenly I recalled having heard perhaps a decade earlier that the pianist of the Boston Symphony, Jesus Maria Sanroma, who had also been "musical secretary" to conductor Serge Koussevitsky, had retired at the latter's death to his native Puerto Rico! I found his name in the telephone directory, called him, and he remembered me as a very young man.

With trembling, I told him of my dilemma, and *dared* to ask him if he would play the week of arduous and dull rehearsals! He readily agreed, and in fact relished the idea of being a part of this project (he had known Leonard Bernstein, the composer, well); his sole condition was that he be allowed to bring one of his piano students to turn pages and a number of them to the dress rehearsal!

Does that answer the question of "where"? Perhaps not; however, it does say that, even in the remotest places, finding the ideal person is not impossible. How can I be more specific? It would seem too obvious to suggest calling the Musicians' Union in the nearest town for a recommendation, or to become friendly with the best piano teacher in town—he might have suggestions, or you might even ask *him* to be good enough to help out in the crisis.

The other question concerns money: "How much should a good rehearsal pianist be paid?" Considering today's fluctuation in all prices, this question will never be answerable. Each region also has a different cost-of-living estimate, and this would make a difference in the pianist's "scale." All things are possible. You may find a superb student-pianist in need of money and you may be mutually helpful by offering him a flat weekly fee for "X" number of weeks (although you may need to work around a schedule to which he is already committed). The sum could be $100 or $150 weekly for four weeks. That could be a godsend to the pianist and to you. But such specific matters have so many ramifications that no one can possibly offer more specific advice, and, indeed, in many nonprofessional theaters no one, not even the various directors, is paid.

If an orchestra is used in this particular production, and the rehearsal pianist is part of it, he can be helpful in a thousand ways, provided he does not try to override the conductor.

At dress rehearsals without orchestra, the general rehearsal pianist should not attempt to play the dance music if another pianist has been rehearsing with the dancers. Otherwise, the tempos will be unnecessarily inexact and there will be innumerable details of which he cannot be aware. If tapes have been employed at rehearsal, they should be used here.

Pianists

The world's greatest pianist would be of no use to the conductor of a musical show—especially at rehearsals—if he were accustomed only to playing solo, and only those pieces he has practiced. The art of accompanying is truly an art. In the theater, the pianist should be one other link in the chain of collaboration.

Chapter 12

Discipline

WHILE THE FOLLOWING WORDS of admonition are addressed to participants in a show, they should also support the directors who may have been given the idea that they were crotchety and lacked proper understanding of the profundity of free youth.

I will go out on a long limb by saying that *all* very successful theater people abide—more or less naturally—by all of the ensuing "directions for using," and that theater cannot possibly exist without a strong sense of discipline. It should provide comfort for director and producer to realize that the "rules" that follow were not voted into existence, but are the results of years of experience, of finding what was needed and what had to be done about it.

When a member of the cast, orchestra, or stage crew enters the stage door (the *only* door he should ever use when he is working in a show), he should be aware of at least two things that have no direct bearing on the show and yet are essential to maximum realization of it:

1. Punctuality (my old aphorism is, "If you aren't at least ten minutes early you are ten minutes late")
2. Quiet, intelligent attentiveness when the stage manager calls, "Places, please"

Both are so obvious that it seems foolish to mention them, and yet, too often, they must be reiterated forcefully. The logic behind them is also obvious: no work can begin when members of the cast are absent. The members who are not present are absent until they are present. If they arrive after the time set for the "call," they have delayed work for everybody because the director has to make one of two choices. First, he can begin with the members who are present, in which case he must take time out of everyone's schedule to explain what the absentee should do, where he should be, and so on. His second choice—also a great waste of time—is to wait until the absent person appears. This kind of situation is needless.

The second axiom—"Quiet, intelligent attention"—has two sides. First, the director (whichever one) needs for his own concentration no distraction—he will be distracted if he "sees" (it is always plainly visible) anyone not giving him his attention, or two people talking together or exchanging notes. This is rude and is bound to cause resentment. If anyone wishes to ask a reasonable question, or wants to make a pertinent observation, he should raise his hand if he is sure he will not be interrupting a train of thought.

If he listens to everything being said, the performer will not fail to carry out the instructions being given. If the performer fails to listen intelligently, the director will immediately comprehend that he was inattentive.

The other side of "paying attention" to *everything* said— whether or not it applies to a particular performer—is that in the end it may very well apply to anyone in the company. What I mean is that someone selected to do a small part may not acquit himself satisfactorily or may sprain an ankle or be called out of town suddenly for some serious reason. The replacement may very well be almost anybody else in the cast. If everyone has listened intelligently, some one person may pleasantly surprise the director as well as his peers, and may have good reason to be proud of himself.

What any director instructs a performer to do, he must *do*. If she is directed to kneel on a stage-floor that is rough and dirty, and the performer happens to be wearing her best stockings, she still must do what is directed. If her stockings are torn, it is her own fault for not having worn the right clothes—work clothes—to rehearsal. The biggest stars bring a change of clothes to rehearsal so that they can do anything required of them, then leave the theater reassuming their "public image."

All of the above items pertain to rehearsals. Very often, in productions on all levels, performers must work *away* from rehearsals: at home, in a hotel room, or anyplace where there is quiet. The player has not been born who is not embarrassed at failure to remember lines. There is only one way to remedy this as far as I know, and that is to work alone and go over whatever has not been firmly entrenched in the brain. This kind of work, away from supervision, requires a very special kind of discipline. If it is done at home, family members must be begged not to interfere. Television that is too loud must be turned down. Telephone calls must not be answered. Since the time between rehearsals—perhaps only this one night—is so short, investment of *this* time, at some loss of sleep, is extremely valuable. If the concentration is intense and the person self-disciplined, the accomplishment will be swifter, easier, and more lasting.

While attention and quiet are essential to the most successful rehearsals, they are even more so at dress rehearsals and, in a different way, at performances.

At dress rehearsal—especially the first—concentrated attention to *everything* is of *mortal* importance. Many performers, even those on Broadway, get "giggly" when they see one another for the first time in wigs, costumes, make-up, and so on. Meanwhile, scenery is being lowered from above or pushed on stage from one side or another. Truly, there is grave danger in not giving undivided attention to everything that happens. A performer can be hit or smashed.

There was a disastrous rehearsal (in Baltimore, I believe) when, instead of one set moving on from left to right, replacing another moving off right at the same time, the wrong buttons were pushed backstage, and *two* sets—one from left and one from right—came on, crushing the middle one. Lights came tumbling down, curtains were pulled in. Fortunately, the performers on stage were alert, saw what must inevitably happen, and all of them leaped into the orchestra pit, the only option they had.

Now, if they had not known what *should* have happened, they couldn't have known until too late what actually *was* happening. Fortunately, no one was hurt in this incident.

There is also the unnecessary interference that unthinking performers can create when stage-hands and prop men are trying to ready a set in a hurry and performers are in the way. The stage manager will surely have told every performer just where it would be safe to wait during every scene change, a place where they would not impede the work of others.

The proper schedule calls for the performer to change into his next costume and its accoutrements as quickly as possible, then return from his dressing room to the side of the stage where he will make his next entrance, observe everything, and be quiet. He may discover that the spot where he chose to wait interferes with others awaiting a momentary entrance.

If he can't make his costume change quickly enough, the performer should go at once to the stage manager to inform him that there is insufficient time for him to make the change alone, and the stage manager will arrange for him to have help. (There is no question of inserting a delay in a performance just to give a performer more time to change a costume.)

In applying make-up, the performer should first be instructed as to what is desirable. This is predicated in the script, which will have told the director the "kind" of character each person is to represent. Is she Hawaiian; did she come from Brooklyn; is he lower-, middle-, or of an elite class? Is he to appear very young or only moderately so? All of these things are first determined by the demands of the script, and tested when the performer is lit.

Next, the director, with the lighting designer, will try to assess the effect of the lights in each particular scene on every character's face. Will the lights be dim or brilliant? Are they blue or predominantly amber? The director or designer will tell the performer to apply more or less make-up accordingly, or perhaps a different kind.

Care should be taken that no members of the ensemble look "far out." Hair-dos also should be the result of instruction from a hair-arrangement professional after he has discussed what is desirable with the stage director. Once the style is set, it should not be altered. The decision is based on a combination of the character being played, the style and period of the show, and the performer's native appearance.

At a dress rehearsal, there is a tendency on everyone's part to want to wander into the auditorium in order to see what everything really looks like: scenery, lights, make-up, costumes, and so on. *Unless* the stage manager has given permission for everyone to do this, all performers must remain discreetly backstage. If anyone is in front (in the auditorium), everyone else should have the same privilege. Even if they are permitted in the auditorium, all performers must be careful to *anticipate* their entrances in the show. If one performer is needed, and he is not positioned backstage, he can cause an unconscionable delay in the rehearsal. (He may become so interested in what he is seeing that he can easily forget to prepare himself for his next entrance.)

Performers in the wings awaiting their next entrances must keep exit spaces clear so that those presently on stage can get off without the need of fighting their way through a wall of other human beings.

Finally, the concentration of a performer awaiting an entrance must be respected. Gratuitous remarks such as "Nice evening" or "You look so pretty" or "I think you're marvelous" are of no interest to a performer preparing to go on stage. This admonition applies equally to a member of the ensemble or the performer of a principal role—the person awaiting an entrance must be left alone. Invading his privacy could distract him and lead to his missing an entrance of forgetting his first line.

Performers should always remember that they are part of a vast whole. They should all listen, watch, and be alert and quiet. Observing these small but important regulations will make a great contribution to the success of the show.

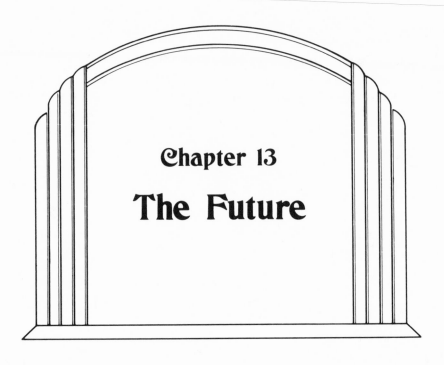

Chapter 13

The Future

IN RECENT YEARS, the regional and nonprofessional theaters have been assuming a number of new roles. About 30 years ago summer musical theaters were autonomous. There were several large ones in St. Louis, Dallas, Pittsburgh, Kansas City, Los Angeles, and many other cities. They generally performed their shows on a weekly basis, which is to say that they presented a different show each week for about 12 weeks during the summer. The star system eventually became the ruling factor, although the specific show (generally revivals) had some effect on attendance.

In addition to the large theaters, which dealt with stars, and had theater-size orchestras (about 25 players) and large ensembles, there were hundreds of others that presented similar shows in smaller theaters accompanied by a piano or a two- or three-piece combo, employed an occasional star, and used small singing-dancing ensembles.

All of these groups—the large and the small—entertained a combined audience of millions each summer.

As the national economy deteriorated, the large theaters found it necessary to work out a plan that would be more beneficial to them (although, by this plan the advantages of competition would then be gone and replaced by a certain inevitable uniformity).

The new benefits resulted from an agreement to book one show in a number of places with the same cast. This meant that the company was required to do less weekly rehearsing, and stars were guaranteed not just *one* week of performance plus a week's rehearsal, but perhaps two or three weeks rehearsal at the start under relatively unhurried conditions, then bookings that included, for example, two weeks in Dallas, one in St. Louis, one in Kansas City, one in Sacramento, and one in Toronto. An entire summer was filled, with less trouble for each city and for the performing company.

In many large places, concert programs by popular performers are replacing some weeks of musical "book" shows. Liza Minnelli, with a small supporting company, has done sellout business. Much earlier, Ethel Merman appeared similarly. Various well-known rock groups have filled a week from time to time in many of these theaters, as have nightclub acts. A "show squeeze" is on.

One reason for having touring companies is to save money and attract more popular stars, which in turn attracts more customers.

But there is a more serious reason. In prior years, Broadway could be counted on annually to offer two or three successful new shows that had completed their runs and were available to summer theaters. During the past several seasons, however, this has not happened. Out of the musicals currently or recently running on Broadway, only *A Chorus Line, Annie, Grease, I Love My Wife, Barnum,* and *Woman of the Year* would be of general interest in the hinterlands, and many of these will not be available for some time.

The past several seasons have seen the largest crop of immediate and expensive failures in the history of musical theater. Most of them lost about two million dollars each. They included *King Of Hearts, Copperfield, A Broadway Musical, Onward Victoria, Charley and Algernon, Bring Back Birdie, Working, Rex, I Remember Mama, Rockabye Hamlet, Runaways,* and others. Many of these were the work of highly respected writers and composers, but there were various kinds of miscalculations and the products simply did not work.

Hence, with no new successful musical shows to be announced in the regional season, rock concerts and similar affairs are essential to filling open weeks and keeping the subscription audience occupied.

Once upon a time, this "filling open weeks" was not a problem, since there was such a wealth of popular "classical" musicals to be done again. But, at least for the moment, summer theater subscribers are thoroughly saturated with *The Student Prince, Desert Song, Rose Marie,* and the Gilbert and Sullivan operettas. The more recent hits have also been done too often in the recent past: *Hello, Dolly!, Cabaret, Oklahoma!, Carousel, The Sound of Music, South Pacific, Funny Girl, Annie Get Your Gun, Gypsy,* and so on. Most other successes of the past two decades have lacked satisfying books and memorable songs that would make them familiar to and popular with the outlying public.

Another change is in the wind and, in my opinion, it will eventually revolutionize the musical theater, regional theaters —large and small—and, finally, Broadway.

Much of this is a result of the colossal increase in production cost, the heightening risk in Broadway investment—two million dollars gone at one roll of the dice, or one edition of three newspapers. The success of *A Chorus Line, Dreamgirls,* and *Nine* and their workshop method of evolution points out the folly of taking that one-night chance unless the product is already tried, previewed for months, rewritten, and given large audiences' stamps of approval. *A Chorus Line* was a big hit *before* the critics were invited to review it. (The workshop method is not infallible, as witnessed by the failure of Michael Bennett's *Ballroom.*)

The present annual paucity of Broadway contribution to the regional and nonprofessional theater exists side by side with the fact that Broadway has never enjoyed greater attendance or taken in more money. At the same time, some producers and their backers have never lost as much money with short-lived extravaganzas—poorly conceived and lavishly produced—many of them never reaching Broadway, others arriving and dying valiantly.

Nevertheless, positive signs emerge. More new writers, composers, directors, choreographers, and performers have had opportunities in the off-off-Broadway theater than ever before. Many of them, seen to advantage, have gone on individually to Broadway. The Hudson Guild sent hits to Broadway: *Da* and *On Golden Pond.* Joseph Papp has sent others besides the indomitable *A Chorus Line* (notably *The Pirates of Penzance*). The Manhattan Theater Club sent a cabaret revue, *Ain't Misbehavin'*, as well as the nonmusical *Crimes of the Heart* and *Mass Appeal.* The Goodspeed Opera House has been represented by *Annie, Going Up, Something's Afoot, Whoopee, Shenandoah, Man of La Mancha,* and *Very Good, Eddie.*

And there have been others from other cities. *Raisin* began performing at the Washington Arena Stage. "The hills are alive with the sound of music" is a lyric, but also a contemporary fact. Each summer a new musical is "read" and discussed at the O'Neill Theater Center in Waterford, Connecticut. Recently, a new musical was fully produced at Colgate University. *Little Shop of Horrors,* a smash hit at the tiny WPA Theater, was re-produced for a run in a much larger theater. All of these and many others have gestated under conditions far less costly and restrictive than a full Broadway production. After they are seen, revised, and possibly seen again, they will hopefully provide union jobs on Broadway and enjoy substantial success.

A Chorus Line and *Annie* are two of Broadway's all-time biggest hits. As with these shows, many others that can now be seen at some distance from New York and under modest circumstances will be sent to Broadway and will return again, under better conditions, to regional and nonprofessional theaters.

What I am saying is that regional theater has taken on a

129

new role. No longer does it base its operation on revival; it now includes—and will continue to do so even more in the future—new works that will feed Broadway and, in time, replenish itself.

Artistically, this will help new writers find their way in a world that has confused many of them and now offers them help in disentangling their careers. Theater, and especially musical theater, has always been an important channel of communication for the human race. What *works* communicates; what does *not* work, fails to communicate.

Regional theater knows that its enormous and varied audiences will welcome what they can relate to. That will be a first test. Corrections can be made. If a new piece of material has any substance and it is improved, there will be other opportunities to revise and try again.

This method is one of encouragement and sanity. Throwing two million dollars in an ash-can overnight because of failure to communicate when there are millions of people who can be reached and asked, "What about it?" is neither sensible nor practical.

I believe we have embarked on our future.

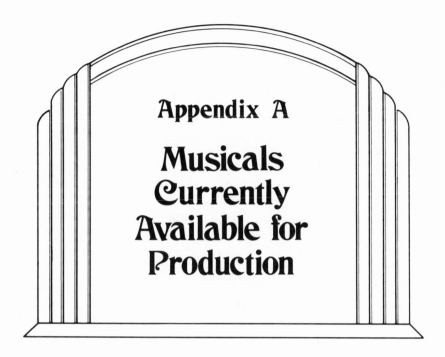

Appendix A

Musicals Currently Available for Production

SOME EXPLANATION of the following list may be helpful. First, the date that follows each title is important. The era in which it was originally produced helps to define the general musical and dramatic styles of the show. Of more vital concern is the fact that, if an orchestra is to be employed in the revival, the producer should become knowledgeable as to the acceptability of the instrumentation to today's audiences. I do not wish to imply that a show, for example, like any of Victor Herbert's should sound like a rock show of the 1960s or 1970s. Such an idea, if put into practice, would destroy the character or quality of the show and its period.* However, without getting into

---

*The successful revival of *The Pirates of Penzance* has new orchestrations using some electronic instruments and no strings. A compromise was achieved, evoking the period sound of the show with contemporary instrumentation.

the rock style of orchestration and its employment of electronic and highly amplified instruments, it must be noted that theater orchestrations before approximately 1935 sound thin to audiences accustomed to the fuller, "fatter" sound of the orchestra after that time. I point this out as a warning.

Lest the foregoing seem unclear, let me note that operatic composers such as Donizetti, and Bellini, Verdi, Puccini, Borodin, Wagner, and Mozart created their own orchestrations, and it would be an act of foolishness to tamper with them. However, in the popular musical theater early in the twentieth century, *arrangers* undertook the job of translating the composers' music into its orchestral components, and there is nothing sacred about the results! Those arrangers accomplished what was best for their time. However, to use an example, Herbert's "Kiss Me Again"—harmonically and melodically—is indestructible, while the original orchestration betrays its time and seems unsatisfying to us today. These orchestrations did not, in any way, fail: they merely manifested their period, while the songs themselves seem to have transcended it.

Returning to the matter of the list, in many cases the number of principals listed is actually more than the number of performers required, since almost invariably performers double parts, and many counted among the characters are taken from the dancing and singing ensembles. Only the number of speaking roles is indicated, not the size of the ensemble.

Similarly, the number of sets listed is almost invariably more than is absolutely essential, especially today. The creative and astute use of lighting can define, limit, and expand playing areas so that a single set, with changed lighting and one or two pieces of furniture, can quite satisfactorily suggest almost any style or place or time that the show represents.

In some cases the choreographer's name is included. To those producers or local dance directors who are *au courant,* this information can be helpful in that it might indicate a special style or technique that colored the original production. If the dancers available locally are insufficiently prepared for work such as that created by Jerome Robbins, Agnes deMille, or Michael Kidd (for example), the dance director can bypass such styles and attempt to create some simpler styles that can be better executed and still achieve a desirable effect.

When the orchestra list is not given, I suggest that the producer write the licensing organization for such information. A majority of nonprofessional theater groups will need to "edit" the orchestral requirements and will know best—individually— how to cope with the original instrumentation.

The "time" designation in each case is employed in an effort to help the local producer—where budgetary problems are stringent—to use contemporary clothes where possible, or to send a warning that such an option is impossible.

The initials next to the year of production of each show in Appendix A refer to the rental agency that handles that particular musical. TW means Tams-Witmark, SF is Samuel French, MTI Music Theater International, and R&H stands for the Rodgers and Hammerstein Library. Addresses of these firms will be found in Chapter 2.

The list that follows is of shows most frequently revived and for which performance materials are most easily obtained.

Allegro (1947) (R&H)

Music by Richard Rodgers

Book and lyrics by Oscar Hammerstein II

Time: 1905–1940, America

Plot: Biography of a man from the time of his birth to his thirty-fifth birthday. He becomes a doctor, marries an ambitious wife, becomes successful, loses his self-respect. At the end, he starts life over again.

Cast: 16 females, 25 males, many of whom are taken from the singing and dancing ensembles; the show employs a Greek-like chorus that comments on the action

Sets: No stage sets (in the conventional sense). Employs small scenic pieces on a moving stage, light projections, and drops.

Choreographer: Agnes deMille

Score includes: "A Fellow Needs a Girl," "So Far," "The Gentleman Is A Dope," "You Are Never Away"

Original Cast Album: RCA Victor (John Battles, Annamary Dickey, Roberta Jonay, John Conte, William Ching)

All in Love (1961) (MTI)

Music by Jacques Urbont

Book and lyrics by Bruce Geller, based on Sheridan's *The Rivals*

Time: 18th-century England

Plot: Story of a comic aunt, Mrs. Malaprop, her niece, and a confusion of lovers and subplots. Farce and comedy.

Cast: Small cast and production

Score includes: "Poor," "What Can It Be?," "All In Love," "Odds," "I Found Him"

Orchestra: Piano, bass, and drums

Original Cast Album: Mercury

Anatol (MTI)

Music by Nancy Ford, based on Themes of Offenbach

Book and lyrics by Tom Jones, based on Schnitzler's *The Affairs of Anatol*

Time: About 1890 (Vienna)

Cast: Romantic comedy for small cast and production

Score includes: "In Vienna," "I Love To Be In Love," "Finishing With An Affair," "Listen to the Rain"

Piano accompaniment

Anne of Green Gables (SF)

Music by Norman Campbell

Book by Donald Harron

Based on L.M. Montgomery's novel, which tells of an orphan girl who rises from destitution to happiness in farm country.

Time: About the turn of the century on Prince Edward Island, Canada

Annie Get Your Gun (1946) (R&H)

Music and lyrics by Irving Berlin

Book by Herbert and Dorothy Fields

Time: Early in the present century

Plot: Concerns a country girl, Annie Oakley, a great sharpshooter

134

who becomes a rage in Buffalo Bill's Wild West Show and nearly loses her lover through her superior marksmanship.

Cast: 20 females, 25 males

Sets: 9

Score includes: "Doin' What Comes Naturally," "The Girl That I Marry," "You Can't Get A Man With A Gun," "There's No Business Like Show Business," "They Say It's Wonderful," "Moonshine Lullaby," "My Defenses Are Down," "I'm An Indian Too," "I Got Lost In His Arms," "Who Do You Love, I Hope," "I Got the Sun in the Morning," "Anything You Can Do"

Original Cast Album: Decca (Ethel Merman, Ray Middleton)

Film Soundtrack: (Betty Hutton, Howard Keel)

Lincoln Center Revival: RCA Victor (Ethel Merman, Bruce Yarnell)

Anyone Can Whistle (1964) (MTI)

Music and lyrics by Stephen Sondheim

Book by Arthur Laurents

Time: Present

Plot: Revolves around a bankrupt town whose council engineers a fake miracle. Water spurts from the rock in the central square. Tourists come to take the miracle waters but the patients from the local sanitarium are refused access. The patients get mixed up with the tourists and no one can tell who is who.

Cast: 7 females, 12 males, and a chorus out of which several identified characters are taken

Sets: 2

Score includes: "Come Play Wiz Me," "Everybody Says Don't," "Simple," "I've Got You To Lean On," "Anyone Can Whistle," "A Parade in Town"

Orchestration: 5 Reeds (each doubling), 2 Horns, 3 Trumpets, 2 Trombones, 2 Percussion, Accordian, 5 Celli, Bass, Piano (celeste)

Original Cast Album: Columbia (Angela Lansbury, Lee Remick, Harry Guardino)

Applause (1970) (TW)

Music by Charles Strouse

Lyrics by Lee Adams

135

Book by Betty Comden and Adolph Green, based on the film *All About Eve*

Plot: Concerns show business, a glamorous star who is made to feel that she is losing her career because of age, and the nudging of a younger performer who is attempting to replace her.

Cast: 6 females, 19 males, many of them double in small parts and are in the singing or dancing ensembles

Sets: 16 scenes (due to repetition, 11 sets)

Choreographer: Ron Field

Score includes: "But Alive," "Applause," "Who's That Girl?," "Fasten Your Seat Belts," "Welcome To The Theater," "One of a Kind"

Orchestra: 5 Reeds (all doubling), 3 Trumpets, 3 Trombones, 2 Percussion, Harp, Electric Organ, Guitar, Piano-celeste, and Strings

Original Cast Album: ABC-Paramount (Lauren Bacall, Len Cariou, Penny Fuller, Bonnie Franklin, Lee Roy Reams)

The Apple Tree (1966) (MTI)

Music by Jerry Bock; lyrics by Sheldon Harnick

Book by Bock and Harnick, based on stories by Mark Twain, Frank R. Stockton, and Jules Feiffer; additional book material by Jerome Coopersmith

These are three one-act plays, unrelated except that each involves a man, a woman, and the supernatural. They were written to be performed together.

Plot: Consists of three one-act musicals: *The Diary of Adam and Eve, The Lady or the Tiger?, Passionella.*

The first is treated with wit and compassion, the second demonstrates the foolishness of love, and the last is about a chimney sweep who becomes a glamorous movie star.

Cast: 2 females, 4 males

Sets: 3 (outside the Garden of Eden, an ancient country, and a rooftop in New York City)

Score includes: "What Makes Me Love Him," "I've Got What You Want," "You Are Not Real," "Oh, To Be a Movie Star"

Orchestra: 5 Reeds (all doubling), 3 Trumpets, 3 Trombones, 1 Horn, 2 Percussion, Guitar, Harp, Piano, and Strings

Original Cast Album: Columbia (Barbara Harris, Alan Alda, Larry Blyden)

136

Babes in Arms (1937) (R&H)

Music by Richard Rodgers

Lyrics by Lorenz Hart

Book by Rodgers and Hart

Revised book by George Oppenheimer

Time: The present

Plot: To save themselves from being sent to a work farm, children of old vaudeville troupers produce a musical revue. It is unsuccessful. Later—because of publicity—they are able to put on a successful show.

Cast: 8 females, 22 males

Sets: 13

Choreographer: George Balanchine

Score includes: "Where or When," "I Wish I Were in Love Again," "My Funny Valentine," "Johnny One Note," "The Lady Is a Tramp"

Studio Record Album: Columbia (Mary Martin, Jack Cassidy)

Baker Street (1965) (TW)

Music and lyrics by Marian Grudeff and Raymond Jessel

Book by Jerome Coopersmith, based on stories by Sir Arthur Conan Doyle

Plot: After Sherlock Holmes helps the musical star Irene Adler retrieve some letters, he discovers she has become infatuated with him. She intrudes into his attempt to prevent Moriarty from stealing Queen Victoria's jewels during the Diamond Jubilee.

Cast: 3 females, 15 males

Sets: 15

Score includes: "It's So Simple," "Leave It To Us, Guv," "Letters," "Finding Words For Spring," "A Married Man," "Jewellery"

Original Cast Album: MGM (Fritz Weaver, Inga Swenson, Virginia Vestoff, Martin Gabel)

Bells Are Ringing (1956) (TW)

Music by Jule Styne

Book and lyrics by Betty Comden and Adolph Green

Plot: Concerns a romance between a telephone answering girl and one of her customers. Neither has seen the other.

Cast: 4 females, 9 males, and smaller parts taken from the ensemble

Sets: 12 (several used more than once)

Score includes: "I Met A Girl," "Long Before I Knew You," "Just In Time," "The Party's Over"

Orchestra: 5 Reeds (all doubling), 2 Horns, 3 Trumpets, 2 Trombones, Percussion, Harp, Piano, Guitar, and Strings

Original Cast Album: Columbia (Judy Holliday, Sydney Chaplin, Jean Stapleton, Eddie Lawrence)

Ben Franklin in Paris (1964) (SF)

Music by Mark Sandrich, Jr.

Book and lyrics by Sidney Michaels

Time: During the reign of Louis XVI

Plot: Franklin as an old man gets Louis XVI to recognize America, and rekindles the passion of a bygone love.

Cast: 4 females, 15 males

Score includes: "Half the Battle," "To Be Alone with You," "You're in Paris," "Look for Small Pleasures"

Original Cast Album: Capitol (Robert Preston, Susan Watson)

Best Foot Forward (1941) (TW)

Music and lyrics by Hugh Martin and Ralph Blane

Book by John Cecil Holm

Time: The 1940s

Plot: At prom time, a college hotshot invites, as a laugh, a Hollywood starlet to be his date, not expecting her to accept. The starlet's press agent sees promotional possibilities and has her accept. The boy's real girl friend is so upset that she rips off the starlet's gown, which sets off a general furor. Avoiding scandal, the starlet returns to Hollywood while the boy and girl are reunited.

Cast: 7 females, 13 males

Sets: 9

Score includes: "Buckle Down, Winsocki," "Ev'ry Time," "What Do You Think I Am?," "Just a Little Joint with a Juke Box"

Revival Cast Album: Cadence (Liza Minnelli, Paula Wayne, Christopher Walken)

138

The Best Little Whorehouse in Texas (1978) (SF)

Music and lyrics by Carol Hall

Book by Larry L. King and Peter Masterson

Time: The present

Plot: A cherished Texas institution comes under attack from moralistic do-gooders.

Cast: 14 females, 15 males, many from the ensemble

Sets: 1

Score includes: "20 Fans," "A Lil' Ole Bitty Pissant Country Place," "Girl You're a Woman," "Texas Has a Whorehouse in It," "Hard Candy Christmas"

Original Cast Album: MCA/Universal (Carlin Glynn, Jay Garner, Dolores Hall, Clint Allmon, Pamela Blair)

Bloomer Girl (1944) (TW)

Music by Harold Arlen

Lyrics by E. Y. Harburg

Book by Sig Herzig and Fred Saidy, based on a play by Dan and Lilith James

Time: Civil War

Plot: Recounts the rebellion of Evelina Applegate, daughter of a hoopskirt manufacturer. She supports her Aunt, Dolly Bloomer, in her campaign to replace hoopskirts with more comfortable "bloomers."

Cast: 12 females, 19 males

Sets: 10 scenes

Choreographer: Agnes deMille

Score includes: "Evelina," "The Eagle and Me," "Right As The Rain," "T'morra, T'morra," "Pretty As A Picture"

Original Cast Album: Decca (Joan McCracken, Celeste Holm, David Brooks, Dooley Wilson, John Call)

The Body Beautiful (1958) (SF)

Music by Jerry Bock

Lyrics by Sheldon Harnick

Book by Joseph Stein and Will Glickman

Time: The present

Plot: Concerns boxing.

Cast: 6 females, 19 males

Sets: 12

Score includes: "Where Are They?," "Fair Warning," "Leave Well Enough Alone," "Just My Luck," "All of These and More"

The Boy Friend (1954) (MTI)

Book, music, and lyrics by Sandy Wilson

Time: the 1920s (a gentle spoof on the musicals of the period)

Plot: An English millionaire's daughter is attending a finishing school and falls in love with a delivery boy who turns out to be the son of a lord. The girl pretends she's a working girl.

Cast: 12 females, 9 males

Sets: 3

Score includes: "The Boy Friend," "I Could Be Happy with You," "Fancy Forgetting," "A Room in Bloomsbury," "It's Never Too Late to Fall in Love," "Poor Little Pierrette"

Orchestra: 3 Reeds (doubling), 2 Trumpets, 1 Trombone, Percussion, Violins A & B, Bass, Banjo, Piano

Original Cast Album: RCA (Julie Andrews)

The Boys from Syracuse (1938) (R&H)

Music by Richard Rodgers

Lyrics by Lorenz Hart

Book by George Abbott, based on Shakespeare's *A Comedy of Errors*

Plot: Confusion with two pairs of twins.

Cast: 9 females, 13 males

Sets: 4

Score includes: "This Can't Be Love," "He and She," "Sing for Your Supper," "Falling in Love with Love," "You Have Cast Your Shadow on the Sea"

Studio Record Album: Columbia (Jack Cassidy, Bibi Osterwald)

Brigadoon (1947) (TW)

Music by Frederick Loewe

Book and lyrics by Alan Jay Lerner

Time: The present and centuries ago

Plot: Two Americans walking through Scotland stumble upon a village which comes to life but one day each century.

Cast: 4 females, 10 males

Sets: 9

Choreography: Agnes deMille

Score includes: "Almost Like Being in Love," "The Heather on the Hill," "There but for You Go I," "Come to Me, Bend to Me," "The Love of My Life"

Orchestra: 5 legitimate Reeds, Horn, 3 Trumpets, 1 Trombone, Percussion, and Strings

Original Cast Album: RCA Victor (David Brooks, Marion Bell, Pamela Britton, Lee Sullivan)

Studio Album: Columbia (Shirley Jones, Jack Cassidy, Susan Johnson)

By Jupiter (1942) (R&H)

Music by Richard Rodgers

Lyrics by Lorenz Hart

Book by Rodgers and Hart, based on Julian Thompson's *The Warrior's Husband*

Time: Ancient Greece

Plot: The women rule. The men invade. When the sword fails, sex succeeds.

Cast: 18 females, 12 males

Sets: 4

Score includes: "Nobody's Heart," "Ev'rything I've Got," "Careless Rhapsody," "Wait Till You See Her"

Revival Cast Album: RCA Victor (Bob Dishy)

By the Beautiful Sea (1954) (MTI)

Music by Arthur Schwartz

Lyrics by Dorothy Fields

Book by Herbert and Dorothy Fields

Time: Early 1900s

Plot: Concerns a vaudevillian who returns to her boarding house after a tour. She accommodates a famous Shakespearean actor with whom she is in love. The presence of his ex-wife makes amusing complications.

Cast: 9 females, 16 males

Score includes: "By The Beautiful Sea," "Happy Habit," "Coney Island Boat," "Alone Too Long," "Old Enough To Love"

Orchestra: 5 Reeds (doubling), 3 Trumpets, 2 Trombones, 2 Horns, Percussion, Piano, and Strings

Original Cast Album: Capitol (Shirley Booth, Wilbur Evans, Mae Barnes)

Bye Bye Birdie (1960) (TW)

Music by Charles Strouse

Lyrics by Lee Adams

Book by Michael Stewart

Time: The 1950s

Plot: Concerns a rock and roll singer (Elvis Presley-type) who is about to be drafted. For publicity, he will bid an all-American teenage girl goodbye. His manager and the manager's longtime girl friend are pivotal characters.

Cast: 14 females, 11 males

Sets: 13

Choreographer: Gower Champion

Score includes: "The Telephone Hour," "How Lovely to Be a Woman," "Put on a Happy Face," "A Lot of Livin' to Do," "Kids," "Baby, Talk to Me"

Orchestra: 4 Reeds (all double), Horn, 3 Trumpets, 2 Trombones, Percussion, Guitar, Piano

Original Cast Album: Columbia (Dick Van Dyke, Chita Rivera, Susan Watson, Paul Lynde)

Cabaret (1966) (TW)

Music by John Kander

Lyrics by Fred Ebb

Book by Joe Masteroff, based on *I Am a Camera* by John van Druten and stories by Christopher Isherwood

Time: Germany, the 1930s

Plot: A young American writer in Hitler's Germany meets Sally Bowles, an English girl who works at the Kit Kat Club. Cliff lives at Fraulein Schneider's house where he is unexpectedly joined by Sally, who has been thrown out by the man she was living with. We see the rise of the Nazis to power, the decadence in the Klub. Cliff wants to take Sally back to America, but she wants to remain in Berlin. On his way home, he begins to write about Sally and Berlin.

Cast: 20 females, 16 males

Sets: 8

Choreographer: Ron Field

Score includes: "Willkommen," "Don't Tell Mama," "Perfectly Marvelous," "Why Should I Wake Up?," "If You Could See Her," "Cabaret"

Orchestra: 4 Reeds (all double), Horn, 2 Trumpets, 2 Trombones, Percussion, Accordian, Celeste, Piano, Guitar, Banjo, Strings, plus stage band: Tenor Saxophone, Trombone, Piano, and Drums

Original Cast Album: Columbia (Joel Grey, Bert Convy, Lotte Lenya, Jack Gilford)

Film Soundtrack: ABC (Liza Minnelli, Joel Grey)

Call Me Madam (1950) (MTI)

Music and lyrics by Irving Berlin

Book by Harold Lindsay and Russel Crouse

Time: Before the present

Plot: Concerns the American Lady Ambassador to Lichtenberg and romantic problems that arise there.

Cast: 6 females, 15 males

Sets: 5

Choreographer: Jerome Robbins

Score includes: "The Hostess With The Mostes' On the Ball," "Marrying For Love," "The Ocarina," "It's a Lovely Day Today," "They Like Ike," "You're Just In Love"

Orchestra: 5 Reeds (all double), 3 Trumpets, 2 Trombones, Percussion, Guitar, Piano, and Strings

Cast Albums: Decca (Ethel Merman with studio cast); RCA Victor (Dinah Shore, Paul Lukas, Russell Nype)

Camelot (1960) (TW)

Music by Frederick Loewe

Book and lyrics by Alan Jay Lerner, based on *The Once And Future King* by T.H. White

Time: The medieval period of the mythical King Arthur

Plot: Concerns King Arthur, his wife Guenevere, and Lancelot.

Cast: 4 females, 15 males

Sets: 17

Choreographer: Hanya Holm

Score includes: "The Simple Joys of Maidenhood," "How To Handle a Woman," "If Ever I Would Leave You," "What Do the Simple Folk Do?," "I Loved You Once In Silence"

Orchestra: 5 Reeds (no saxophones), 3 Horns, 3 Trumpets, 2 Trombones, Percussion, Guitar (Lute and Mandolin), Harp, Piano, and Strings.

Original Cast Album: Columbia (Richard Burton, Julie Andrews, and Robert Goulet)

Film Soundtrack: Warner Bros.

Can-Can (1953) (TW)

Music and lyrics by Cole Porter

Book by Abe Burrows

Plot: In Paris, a young magistrate goes to investigate charges of the immorality of the Can-Can and falls in love with the proprietress of the cafe where the dancing is done. He is disbarred and joins his love in teaching the Can-Can.

Cast: 8 females, 26 males, many of the men taken from the ensemble

Sets: 6

Choreographer: Michael Kidd

Score includes: "C'est Magnifique," "Live and Let Live," "I Love Paris," "Allez-Vous En," "It's All Right With Me"

Original Cast Album: Capitol (Lilo, Peter Cookson, Hans Conried, Gwen Verdon, Erik Rhodes)

Film Soundtrack: (Frank Sinatra, Shirley MacLaine, Maurice Chevalier, Louis Jourdan)

144

Candide (1956 revival) (MTI)

Music by Leonard Bernstein

Lyrics by Richard Wilbur, Stephen Sondheim, and John LaTouche

Book by Hugh Wheeler, adapted from Voltaire's novel

Time: The middle ages

Plot: Dr. Pangloss prepares his young charges for a life of philosophy in a world of virtue. All of them, including Candide and Cunegonde, his love, go through every possible disaster, and through it all, Candide continues to believe, "This is the best of all possible worlds."

Cast: 10 females, 28 males

Sets: 9

Score includes: "The Best Of All Possible Worlds," "Glitter and Be Gay," "Auto Da Fe, "My Love"

Orchestra: 1 Flute, 2 Clarinets, 2 Trumpets, Trombone, Drums, 2 Pianos, and Strings (this is the revised version)

Original Cast Album: Columbia (Barbara Cook, Robert Rounseville, Max Adrian, William Chapman, Irra Petina)

Canterbury Tales (1969) (MTI)

Music by Richard Hill and John Hawkins

Lyrics by Nevill Coghill

Book by Martin Starkie and Nevill Coghill, based on the works of Geoffrey Chaucer

Time: Chaucer's England (14th Century)

Plot: A medley of four of Chaucer's tales, from the travelers' first meeting at the Tabard Inn, throughout their journey to Canterbury.

Cast: 5 females, 14 males

Sets: 4

Score includes: "Canterbury Day," "Love Will Conquer All," "Come On and Marry Me Honey," "If She Has Never Loved Before"

Orchestra: 3 Trumpets, Horn, 2 Trombones, 2 Guitars, Bass, 2 Percussion, Piano (with Electric Organ)

Original Cast Album: Capitol Records (Martyn Green, Hermione Baddeley, George Rose, Sandy Duncan, Ed Evanko)

Carnival (1961) (TW)

Music and lyrics by Bob Merrill

Book by Michael Stewart, based on material by Helen Deutsch

Time: A few years ago

Plot: Lili, an orphan, is unsuccessful in several jobs with the circus troupe and becomes the pawn in a rivalry for her affection between the troupe's magician and the puppeteer with a game leg.

Cast: 7 females, 10 males

Sets: 8

Choreographer: Gower Champion

Score includes: "Love Makes the World Go Round," "Fairyland," "Sword, Rose and Cape," "Mira," "Her Face"

Orchestra: 5 Reeds (all double), Horn, 2 Trumpets, 2 Trombones, 2 Percussion, Harp, Guitar, Accordian, Piano (Celeste), and Strings

Original Cast Album: MGM (Pierre Olaf, Anita Gillette, James Mitchell, Kaye Ballard, Jerry Orbach, Anna Maria Alberghetti)

Carousel (1945) (R&H)

Music by Richard Rodgers

Book and lyrics by Oscar Hammerstein II, based on *Liliom* by Ferenc Molnar

Time: 1873 (the coast of Maine)

Plot: Concerns the love of Julie Jordan and Billy Bigelow even after the latter's death.

Cast: 5 females, 4 males

Sets: 9

Choreographer: Agnes deMille

Score includes: "If I Loved You," "You'll Never Walk Alone," "June Is Bustin' Out All Over," "Soliloquy"

Original Cast Album: Decca (Jan Clayton and John Raitt)

Film Soundtrack: Capitol (Gordon MacRae, Shirley Jones)

Lincoln Center Cast: RCA Victor (Eileen Christy, John Raitt)

Studio Recording: RCA Victor (Robert Merrill and Patrice Munsel)

Celebration (1969) (MTI)

Music by Tom Jones

Book and lyrics by Harvey Schmidt

Time: Abstract, suggestive of the present.

Plot: A comedic ritual about an ancient battle between an old man and a young one set on New Year's Eve—played out with masks and torches. It is an allegory about a young orphan looking for his lost garden of beautiful Peace, who becomes entangled with bizarre characters including the richest man in the world and a fallen angel.

Cast: 1 female, 3 males

Sets: 1

Score includes: "My Garden," "Celebration," "Somebody," "Where Did It Go?," "Love Song"

Orchestra: 2 Pianos and Percussion, plus Guitar, Bass, Harp, Electric Piano (which may be omitted)

Original Cast Album: Capitol Records (Susan Watson, Keith Charles, Ted Thurston, Michael Glenn-Smith)

Company (1970) (MTI)

Music and lyrics by Stephen Sondheim

Book by George Furth

Time: The present

Plot: An unmarried young man, adored by his married friends and several unmarried girls, finally does want someone.

Cast: 8 females, 6 males

Sets: 1 basic set with slides

Choreographer: Michael Bennett

Score includes: "Company," "Little Things," "Another Hundred People," "Side By Side," "Barcelona," "The Ladies Who Lunch"

Orchestra: 5 Reeds (all double), 3 Trumpets, 2 Trombones, Electric Keyboard, 2 Guitars, 2 Percussion, and Strings (instrumentation may be reduced) 4 female voices (minimum)

Original Cast Album: Columbia (Dean Jones, Barbara Barrie, Elaine Stritch, Pamela Myers, Donna McKechnie)

The Contrast (SF)

Music by Don Pippin

Lyrics by Steve Brown

Book by Anthony Stimac, adapted from Royall Tyler's play

Time: 18th century

Plot: Contrasts those early Americans who decked themselves in powdered wigs and knee britches, and those more rough and ready countrymen.

Dames at Sea (1968) (SF)

Music by Jim Wise

Book and lyrics by George Haimsohn and Robin Miller

Time: The 1930s

Plot: A parody on Hollywood musicals of the thirties.

Cast: 3 females, 4 males

Sets: 2

Score includes: "Wall Street," "It's You," "That Mister Man of Mine," "Choo-Choo Honeymoon"

Original Cast Album: Columbia (Bernadette Peters, Tamara Long, Sally Stark, Steve Elmore)

Damn Yankees (1955) (MTI)

Music and lyrics by Richard Adler and Jerry Ross

Book by George Abbott and Douglass Wallop, based on *The Year the Yankees Lost the Pennant,* by Douglass Wallop

Plot: Concerns a fanatic Washington Senators' fan who says he would sell his soul if he could stop the Yankees. A happily cynical Devil appears and the fan is transformed into a young, long-ball hitter—something the Senators need.

Cast: 7 females, 13 males

Sets: 17

Choreographer: Bob Fosse

Score includes: "Whatever Lola Wants," "Heart," "Who's Got the Pain"

Orchestra: 5 Reeds (all double), 3 Trumpets, 3 Trombones, Horn, Percussion, Guitar, Piano, and Strings.

148

Original Cast Album: RCA Victor (Gwen Verdon, Stephen Douglass, Shannon Bolin, Ray Walston, Rae Allen)

Dear World (1969) (TW)

Music and lyrics by Jerry Herman

Book by Jerome Lawrence and Robert E. Lee, based on *The Madwoman of Chaillot* by Jean Giraudoux

Time: The present (Paris)

Plot: Three madwomen confound the same rich man and help the course of true love.

Cast: 4 females, 10 males

Score includes: "Each Tomorrow Morning," "I Don't Want to Know," "I've Never Said I Love You," "And I Was Beautiful"

Original Cast Album: Columbia (Angela Lansbury, Jane Connell, Carmen Matthews, Kurt Peterson, Milo O'Shea)

Dearest Enemy (1925) (R&H)

Music by Richard Rodgers

Lyrics by Lorenz Hart

Book by Herbert Fields

Time: 1776

Plot: The British have landed in New York and only a woman's charm can save the surrounded regiment.

Cast: 6 females, 11 males

Sets: 3

Score includes: "Here in My Arms," "War is War," "I Beg Your Pardon," "Bye and Bye"

Destry Rides Again (1959) (TW)

Music and lyrics by Harold Rome

Book by Leonard Gershe, based on the story by Max Brand

Time: Before the turn of the century

Plot: A mild-spoken lawman is enlisted to break the corrupt stranglehold an outlaw gang has on a wild west town. There is a romance between him and a girl associated with the outlaws.

Cast: 6 females, 14 males

Sets: 8

Choreographer: Michael Kidd

Score includes: "Hoop-Di-Dingle," "Ballad of the Gun," "I Know Your Kind," "Anyone Would Love You," Once Knew a Fella," "Fair Warning," "I Say Hello"

Original Cast Album: Decca (Dolores Gray, Andy Griffith, Elizabeth Watts, Nolan Van Way)

Do I Hear a Waltz? (1965) (R&H)

Music by Richard Rodgers

Lyrics by Stephen Sondheim

Book by Arthur Laurents, based on Mr. Laurents' play *The Time of the Cuckoo*

Time: The present

Plot: Concerns an unmarried American secretary "of a certain age" who takes her first trip to Venice, where she meets a suave man of approximately her own age who is married; her illusions come into conflict with reality.

Cast: 6 females, 6 males

Sets: 6

Score includes: "Someone Woke Up," "Take the Moment," "Someone Like You," "No Understand," "Moon in My Window," "We're Gonna Be All Right"

Orchestra: 4 Reeds (double, but no Saxophones), 2 Trumpets, 3 Trombones, Percussion, Harp, Celeste, Guitar/Mandolin, and Strings

Original Cast Album: Columbia (Sergio Franchi, Elizabeth Allen, Carol Bruce)

Do Re Mi (1960) (TW)

Music by Jule Styne

Lyrics by Betty Comden and Adolph Green

Book By Garson Kanin

Time: The present

Plot: A comedy involving a ne'er-do-well who becomes involved with gangsters in the juke box business.

Cast: 10 females, 16 males

Sets: 13

Score includes: "Waiting," "Take a Job," "Cry Like The Wind," "Fireworks," "What's New At The Zoo?," "Adventure," "Make Someone Happy"

Original Cast Album: RCA Victor (Phil Silvers, Nancy Walker, Nancy Dussault, John Reardon, David Burns)

Fade Out-Fade In (1964) (TW)

Music by Jule Styne

Book and lyrics by Betty Comden and Adolph Green

Time: The present (Hollywood)

Plot: An unpromising chorus girl is accidentally starred in a new film which, eventually, is a success.

Cast: 11 females, 21 males

Score includes: "Fear," "Call Me Savage," "The Usher from the Mezzanine," "You Mustn't Be Discouraged," "Fade Out-Fade In"

Original Cast Album: ABC-Paramount (Carol Burnett, Jack Cassidy, Tina Louise)

A Family Affair (1962) (MTI)

Music by John Kander

Book and lyrics by James and William Goldman

Plot: The complications that arise out of an engagement and wedding of a couple because of their families' preferences.

Cast: 18 females, 13 males, many also in the ensemble

Score includes: "My Son, the Lawyer," "There's a Room in My House," "Harmony," "Summer Is Over," "Revenge," "Wonderful Party"

Original Cast Album: United Artists (Rita Gardner, Larry Kert, Eileen Heckart, Linda Lavin, Morris Carnovsky, Bibi Osterwald)

Fanny (1954) (TW)

Music and lyrics by Harold Rome

Book by S. N. Behrman and Joshua Logan, based on the *Marius, Fanny,* and *Cesar* trilogy by Marcel Pagnol

Time: "Not so long ago"

Plot: Concerns a boy who loves the sea more than the girl who loves him and the complications of his leave-taking and her pregnancy.

Cast: 10 females, 18 males

Sets: 14

Score includes: "Never Too Late For Love," "Restless Heart," "Why Be Afraid To Dance?," "Panisse and Son," "To My Wife," "Love Is A Very Light Thing," "Fanny"

Original Cast Album: RCA Victor (Ezio Pinza, Walter Slezak, Florence Henderson, William Tabbert)

The Fantasticks (1960) (MTI)

Music by Harvey Schmidt

Book and lyrics by Tom Jones, suggested by Rostand's *Les Romantiques*

Time: The present

Plot: Concerns young love, parents, the world, and human nature.

Cast: 1 female, 8 males

Set: 1

Score includes: "Try To Remember," "Much More," "Soon It's Gonna Rain," "I Can See It," "They Were You"

Orchestra: Piano and Harp

Original Cast Album: MGM (Jerry Orbach, Rita Gardner, Kenneth Nelson)

Fiddler on the Roof (1964) (MTI)

Music by Jerry Bock

Lyrics by Sheldon Harnick

Book by Joseph Stein, based on stories by Sholom Aleichem

Time: About 1900

Plot: Concerns a Jewish community and one family in particular in Russia, 1905, and the disintegration of tradition.

Cast: 10 females, 12 males

Sets: 13

Choreographer: Jerome Robbins

Score includes: "Tradition," "Matchmaker," "If I Were a Rich Man,"

"Miracle of Miracles," "Sunrise, Sunset," "Do You Love Me?," "Far From The Home I Love"

Orchestra: 5 Reeds (no Saxophones), 3 Trumpets, 1 Trombone, Horn, Accordian, Guitar, Percussion, Piano, and Strings (some of these may be eliminated)

Original Cast Album: RCA Victor (Zero Mostel, Maria Karnilova, Julia Migenes, Beatrice Arthur, Austin Pendleton, Bert Convy)

Finian's Rainbow (1947) (TW)

Music by Burton Lane

Lyrics by E. Y. Harburg

Book by E. Y. Harburg and Fred Saidy

Time: Before the present

Plot: A fantasy and an allegory about an Irish immigrant and his daughter who come to America to get rich, on the theory that the soil at Fort Knox radiates gold.

Cast: 5 females, 23 males

Choreographer: Michael Kidd

Score includes: "How Are Things In Glocca Morra?," "Look To The Rainbow," "Old Devil Moon," "If This Isn't Love"

Orchestra: 5 Reeds (no Saxophones), 2 Horns, 2 Trumpets, 2 Trombones, Percussion, Harp, Piano-Celeste, Guitar-Banjo, and Strings

Original Cast Album: Columbia (Ella Logan, Donald Richards, David Wayne)

Fiorello! (1959) (TW)

Music by Jerry Bock

Lyrics by Sheldon Harnick

Book by Jerome Weidman and George Abbott

Time: The 1930s

Plot: From the biography of Fiorello H. LaGuardia, mayor of New York City.

Cast: 6 females, 21 males

Sets: 13

Score includes: "On the Side of the Angels," "Till Tomorrow," "Politics and Poker," "Marie's Law," "I Love A Cop," "When Did I Fall In Love?," "Little Tin Box"

Original Cast Album: Capitol Records (Tom Bosley, Pat Stanley, Howard Da Silva, Ellen Hanley, Patricia Wilson)

First Impressions (1959) (SF)

Music and lyrics by Robert Goldman, Glenn Paxton, and George Weiss

Book by Abe Burrows, adapted from Jane Austen's *Pride and Prejudice* and the play by Helen Jerome

Time: 18th-century England

Plot: The marrying off of Mrs. Bennet's five daughters.

Cast: 11 females, 11 males

Sets: 9

Score includes: "A Perfect Evening," "A House in Town," "The Heart Has Won the Game," "Wasn't It a Simply Lovely Wedding?," "Love Will Find Out the Way"

Original Cast Album: Columbia (Hermione Gingold, Phyllis Newman, Polly Bergen, Ellen Hanley, Marti Stevens, Donald Madden, Farley Granger)

Flower Drum Song (1958) (R&H)

Music by Richard Rodgers

Lyrics by Oscar Hammerstein II

Book by Hammerstein and Joseph Fields, based on C. Y. Lee's novel

Time: The present

Plot: Concerned with conflicts between the old and new China. The story centers about a "mail-order" bride who is brought to San Francisco to marry a thoroughly Americanized Chinese youth and the complications that arise.

Cast: 7 females, 11 males

Sets: 10

Score includes: "You Are Beautiful," "A Hundred Million Miracles," "I Enjoy Being A Girl," "I Am Going To Like It Here," "Love, Look Away," "Don't Marry Me"

Orchestra: 6 Reeds (all double), 3 Trumpets, 2 Trombones, Tuba, Percussion, Harp, Guitar (Banjo and Mandolin)

Original Cast Album: Columbia (Ed Kenney, Pat Suzuki, Larry Blyden, Miyoshi Umeki, Arabella Hong)

Follies (1971) (MTI)

Music and lyrics by Stephen Sondheim

Book by James Goldman

Time: The present

Plot: A reunion given by a theater-owner at his theater before it becomes a parking lot—"to stumble through a song or 2 and lie about ourselves a little." The theater is filled with performers from the producer's *Follies* in addition to the ghosts of elegantly costumed show girls. Two unhappily married couples make a last frantic attempt to relive their pasts so that they may cope with the present. There are follies numbers—thrilling and eerie as the aging performers mingle with their younger selves.

Cast: 51

Set: An empty stage that is filled with bits of scenery, past and present

Choreographer: Michael Bennett

Score includes: "Beautiful Girls," "Waiting for the Girls Upstairs," "Broadway Baby," "I'm Still Here," "Too Many Mornings," "Losing My Mind," "Could I Leave You?"

Orchestra: 5 Reeds (doubling), Horn, 3 Trumpets, 3 Trombones, Strings, Harp, Percussion, Piano

Original Cast Album: Capitol (Dorothy Collins, Yvonne DeCarlo, Alexis Smith, John McMartin, Kurt Peterson, Gene Nelson)

Funny Girl (1964) (TW)

Music by Jule Styne

Lyrics by Bob Merrill

Book by Isobel Lennart

Time: Before and after World War I

Plot: Built around the life of Fanny Brice

Cast: 15 females, 19 males

Sets: 15

Score includes: "I'm the Greatest Star," "His Love Makes Me Beautiful," "Henry Street," "People," "Don't Rain On My Parade"

Orchestra: 5 Reeds (all double), Horn, 3 Trumpets, 3 Trombones, Percussion, Guitar, Piano with Celeste and Strings.

Original Cast Album: Columbia (Barbra Streisand, Kay Medford, Jean Stapleton, Sydney Chaplin)

A Funny Thing Happened on the Way to the Forum (1962) (MTI)

Music and lyrics by Stephen Sondheim

Book by Burt Shevelove and Larry Gelbart, based on plays by Plautus

Time: Ancient Rome

Plot: Concerns the conniving of a slave to achieve his freedom. Hilarious vaudeville style.

Cast: 8 females, 8 males

Set: 1

Choreographer: Jack Cole

Score includes: "Comedy Tonight," "Free," "Love, I Hear," "Lovely," "Everybody Ought To Have A Maid"

Orchestra: 5 Reeds (all double), 3 Trumpets, 3 Trombones, Percussion, Harp, and Strings.

Original Cast Album: Capitol (Zero Mostel, David Burns, Ruth Kobart, Brian Davies, Jack Gilford, Preshy Marker)

George M! (1968) (TW)

Music and lyrics by George M. Cohan

Book by Michael Stewart and John and Fran Pascal

Time: About 1900

Plot: based on the life of George M. Cohan.

Cast: 11 females, 12 males

Sets: 17

Score includes: "All Aboard for Broadway," "Give My Regards to Broadway," "45 Minutes From Broadway," "Mary," "Yankee Doodle Dandy"

Orchestra: 5 Reeds (no Saxophones), Horn, 3 Trumpets, 2 Trombones, Percussion, Piano-Celeste, and Strings

Original Cast Album: Columbia (Joel Grey, Jill O'Hara, Bernadette Peters, Jonelle Allen)

156

Gigi (1973) (TW)

Music by Frederick Loewe

Book and lyrics by Alan Jay Lerner, based on a novel by Colette

Time: Turn of the century, Paris

Plot: Concerns an extremely wealthy young man-about-town who, after many meaningless affairs, falls in love and finally marries the young girl, Gigi.

Cast: 4 females, 14 males

Score includes: "Thank Heaven for Little Girls," "She is Not Thinking of Me," "The Night They Invented Champagne," "I'm Glad I'm Not Young Anymore"

Orchestra: 5 Reeds (no Saxophone), 2 Horns, 3 Trumpets, 2 Trombones, 2 Percussion, Harp, Piano-Celeste, and Strings

Original Cast Album: RCA Victor (Alfred Drake, Daniel Massey, Maria Karnilova, Karin Wolfe, Agnes Moorehead)

The Golden Apple (1954) (TW)

Music by Jerome Moross

Book and lyrics by John LaTouche, based on Homer's *The Odyssey*

Time: 1900–1910

Plot: Built on the Ulysses legend but set in Washington State between 1900 and 1910.

Cast: 6 females, 18 males

Choreographer: Hanya Holm

Score includes: "It's the Going Home Together," "Windflowers," "Helen Is Always Willing," "Lazy Afternoon," "My Picture in the Papers"

Original Cast Album: Elektra (Kaye Ballard, Bibi Osterwald, Portia Nelson, Priscilla Gillette, Stephen Douglass, Jack Whiting)

Golden Boy (1964) (SF)

Music by Charles Strouse

Lyrics by Lee Adams

Book by William Gibson and Clifford Odets, based on the play by Clifford Odets

Time: The present

Plot: Concerns a young prize-fighter who rises from Harlem to fame in the brutal white world.

Cast: 2 females, 9 males

Sets: 17

Score includes: "Night Song," "Stick Around," "Lorna's Here," "This Is the Life," "Golden Boy," "I Want To Be with You"

Original Cast Album: Capitol (Sammy Davis, Jr., Paula Wayne, Billy Daniels)

Golden Rainbow (1968) (SF)

Music and lyrics by Walter Marks

Book by Ernest Kinoy, based on the play *A Hole in the Head* by Arnold Schulman

Time: The Present

Plot: Set in Las Vegas—a father who is a dreamer, a girl who thinks she is a realist, and a boy who loves them both.

Cast: 8 females, 16 males

Sets: 11

Score includes: "Golden Rainbow," "We Got Us," "He Needs Me Now," "I've Got To Be Me"

Original Cast Album: Columbia (Steve Lawrence, Eydie Gorme, Marilyn Cooper, Fay Sappington)

Goldilocks (1958) (SF)

Music by Leroy Anderson

Lyrics by Walter and Jean Kerr and Joan Ford

Book by Jean Kerr and Walter Kerr

Time: Early days of the silent films

Plot: Deals with a movie producer who wants to make a big spectacle set in Egypt, and his locking horns with his leading lady.

Cast: 3 females, 8 males

Sets: 10

Choreographer: Agnes deMille

Score includes: "Lazy Moon," "No One'll Ever Love You," "Who's Been Sitting in My Chair?," "The Pussy Foot," "I Never Know When"

Original Cast Album: Columbia (Elaine Stritch, Don Ameche, Russell Nype, Pat Stanley)

The Grass Harp (1971) (SF)

Music by Claibe Richardson

Book and lyrics by Kenward Elmslie, based on Truman Capote's novel and play

Time: The past

Plot: "Once upon a time, a band of gypsies entrusted a secret elixir to a Southern lady whose greedy sister tried to parlay it into riches."

Cast: 5 females, 4 males

Sets: 2

Score includes: "This One Day," "Yellow Drum," "If There's Love Enough," "Walk Into Heaven," "Take a Little Sip," "Reach Out," "Chain of Love"

Original Cast Album: Painted Smiles (Barbara Cook, Russ Thacker, Carol Brice, Ruth Ford, Karen Morrow, Max Showalter)

Grease (1972) (SF)

Music, lyrics, and book by Jim Jacobs and Warren Casey

Time: The late 1950s

Plot: A spoof, or perhaps re-creation, of high school life in the 1950s.

Cast: 6 females, 9 males

Sets: 12

Choreographer: Patricia Birch

Score includes: "Summer Nights," "Look At Me, I'm Sandra Dee," "There Are Worse Things I Could Do," "Beauty School Dropout," "It's Raining on Prom Night," "Alone at the Drive-in Movie," "All Choked Up"

Original Cast Album: MGM (Barry Bostwick, Walter Bobbie, Adrienne Barbeau, Carole Demas)

Guys and Dolls (1950) (MTI)

Music and lyrics by Frank Loesser
Book by Jo Swerling and Abe Burrows, based on stories and characters by Damon Runyon

Time: The recent past

Plot: Tells of a lady "soul-saver" and her unintentional love for a professional gambler; also a singer in a saloon and her 14-year engagement to another gambler.

Cast: 6 females, 14 males

Sets: 12

Choreographer: Michael Kidd

Score includes: "Fugue for Tinhorns," "I'll Know," "Adelaide's Lament," "Guys And Dolls," "If I Were A Bell," "I've Never Been In Love Before," "Luck Be A Lady"

Orchestra: 5 Reeds (all doubles), 3 Trumpets, 1 Trombone, Horn, Percussion, Piano, and Strings

Original Cast Album: Decca (Stubby Kaye, Isabel Bigley, Pat Rooney, Sr., Sam Levene, Vivian Blaine, Robert Alda)

Gypsy (1959) (TW)

Music by Jule Styne

Lyrics by Stephen Sondheim

Book by Arthur Laurents, suggested by memoirs of Gypsy Rose Lee

Time: Early 1920s to early 1930s

Plot: Centers around the early lives of Gypsy Rose Lee, her mother, and sister, and Gypsy's eventual success and reconciliation with her mother.

Cast: 16 females, 13 males

Sets: 17

Choreographer: Jerome Robbins

Score includes: "Let Me Entertain You," "Some People," "Small World," "Mr. Goldstone," "If Momma Was Married," "Everything's Coming up Roses," "Together Wherever We Go," "Rose's Turn"

Original Cast Album: Columbia (Ethel Merman, Jack Klugman, Sandra Church, Lane Bradbury)

Hair (1968) (TW)

Music by Galt MacDermot

Book and lyrics by Gerome Ragni and James Rado

Time: The period of the Viet Nam War

Plot: Concerns the "Flower Children," the generation of the sixties, and the shadow of the Viet Nam War. In a conventional sense, there was very little plot.

Cast: 11 females, 11 males

Set: 1 (with onstage changes)

Score includes: "I Got Life," "Frank Mills," "Where Do I Go?," "Manchester," "Aquarius," "Good Morning Starshine"

Cast Album: RCA Victor (Ronald Dyson, Gerome Ragni, Steve Curry, Lamont Washington, James Rado, Shelley Plimpton, Lynn Kellogg)

Hallelujah, Baby! (1967) (MTI)

Music by Jule Styne

Lyrics by Betty Comden and Adolph Green

Book by Arthur Laurents

Time: The present

Plot: The poignant story of a young black girl, her mother, and boyfriend as they meet the social problems in our society that have prevailed over the past 60 years. The story progresses from decade to decade, but an unusual twist is that none of the characters gets any older.

Cast: 22

Sets: 6

Orchestra: 5 Reeds (with doubles), 3 Trumpets, 1 Horn, 3 Trombones, 2 Percussion, Guitar (or Banjo), Violins, Celli, Bass, Piano

Score includes: "My Own Morning," "Talking to Yourself," "Not Mine," "Watch My Dust," "Hallelujah, Baby!"

Original Cast Album: Columbia (Leslie Uggams, Lillian Hayman, Robert Hooks, Allen Case, Barbara Sharma, Frank Hamilton, Marilyn Cooper)

Happy Hunting (1956) (MTI)

Music by Harold Karr

Lyrics by Matt Dubey

Book by Howard Lindsay and Russel Crouse

Time: The recent past

Plot: A wealthy Philadelphia socialite feels she has been snubbed at the Kelly-Rainier wedding and sets out to get a titled Spaniard for her daughter. The mother falls in love with her royal Duke and all works out happily.

Cast: 9 females, 21 males

Sets: 16

Score includes: "Mutual Admiration Society," "Don't Tell Me," "It's Like a Beautiful Woman," "Mr. Livingstone," "If'n," "A New-Fangled Tango"

Orchestra: 5 Reeds (all double), 3 Trumpets, 2 Trombones, Horn, Percussion, Guitar, Piano, and Strings

Original Cast Album: RCA Victor (Ethel Merman, Fernando Lamas, Gordon Polk, Virginia Gibson)

Hello, Dolly! (1964) (TW)

Music and lyrics by Jerry Herman

Book by Michael Stewart, based on Thornton Wilder's play *The Matchmaker*

Time: About the turn of the century

Plot: Concerns Dolly Levi, a widow who maneuvers everyone's lives and ends with a wealthy marriage for herself.

Cast: 6 females, 7 males

Sets: 8

Choreographer: Gower Champion

Score includes: "It Takes a Woman," "Put on Your Sunday Clothes," "Hello, Dolly!," "Before the Parade Passes By," "It Only Takes a Moment"

Orchestra: 4 Reeds (all double), 3 Trumpets, 2 Trombones, 2 Percussion, Guitar-Banjo, Piano-Celeste, and Strings

Original Cast Album: RCA Victor (Carol Channing, David Burns, Charles Nelson Reilly, Eileen Brennan, Gordon Connell)

Henry, Sweet Henry (1967) (SF)

Music and lyrics by Bob Merrill

Book by Nunnally Johnson, based on the novel *The World of Henry Orient* by Nora Johnson

Time: The present

Plot: Two teenage girls set out to follow Henry Orient, avant-garde composer and the man of their dreams, everywhere.

Cast: 6 females, 9 males

Sets: 16

Score includes: "In Some Little World," "Here I Am," "Nobody Steps on Kafritz," "Henry, Sweet Henry," "Weary Near To Dyin' "

Original Cast Album: ABC-Paramount (Don Ameche, Carol Bruce, Alice Playten)

Here's Love! (1963) (MTI)

Music, lyrics, and book by Meredith Willson, based on the film *Miracle on 34th Street*

Time: The recent past

Plot: Has to do with a modern mother who wants to protect her daughter from the clichés of modern life and her unintentional mix-up with a department store Santa Claus.

Cast: 8 females, 14 males

Score includes: "Here's Love!," "Pine Cones and Holly Berries," "My Wish," "Hand-In-Hand," "Look, Little Girl," "That Man Over There"

Orchestra: 5 Reeds (all double), 3 Trumpets, 3 Trombones, Horn, Percussion, Celeste, Guitar, Piano, and Strings

Original Cast Album: Columbia (Laurence Naismith, Craig Stevens, Janis Paige, Larry Douglas, Kathy Cody)

High Button Shoes (1947) (TW)

Music and lyrics by Jule Styne and Sammy Cahn

Book by Stephen Longstreet

Time: 1913

Plot: Concerns two madcap crooks who are constantly foiled by their own stupidity.

Cast: 6 females, 14 males

Sets: 2

Choreographer: Jerome Robbins

Score includes: "On a Sunday by the Sea," "I Still Get Jealous," "Can't You Just See Yourself In Love With Me?," "Next to Texas, I Love You," "Papa, Won't You Dance With Me?"

Original Cast Album: Camden (Phil Silvers, Joey Faye, Nanette Fabray, Helen Gallagher, Arthur Partington, Sondra Lee)

High Spirits (1964) (TW)

Music, lyrics, and book by Hugh Martin and Timothy Gray, based on Noel Coward's *Blithe Spirit*

Time: The present

Plot: Concerns an "incomparable spiritualist" who brings the hero's first wife back from the grave at the celebration of his second wedding, and the complications that result.

Cast: 6 females, 4 males

Sets: 5

Score includes: "Was She Prettier Than I?," "You'd Better Love Me," "The Bicycle Song," "Where Is the Man I Married?," "Home Sweet Heaven," "Something Is Coming to Tea"

Original Cast Album: ABC-Paramount (Beatrice Lillie, Tammy Grimes, Edward Woodward, Louise Troy)

How Now, Dow Jones (1967) (SF)

Music by Elmer Bernstein

Lyrics by Carolyn Leigh

Book by Max Shulman

Time: The present

Plot: Concerns a hayseed who stumbles into Wall Street and fails. He meets a pretty girl who reads the Dow Jones Averages over the radio daily. He says he'll marry her when the Average exceeds 1000. As she becomes pregnant, she hastens her wedding day by falsely reporting extra-high averages. The situation is, of course, resolved.

Cast: 8 females, 21 males

Sets: 11

Score includes: "Live A Little," "The Pleasure's About to Be Mine," "Walk Away," "Step to the Rear," "Big Trouble," "He's Here!"

Original Cast Album: RCA (Brenda Vaccaro, Anthony Roberts, Hiram Sherman, Marilyn Mason)

How To Succeed in Business Without Really Trying (1961) (MTI)

Music and lyrics by Frank Loesser

Book by Abe Burrows, Jack Weinstock and Willie Gilbert, based on the novel by Shepherd Mead

Time: The present

Plot: A farce—concerns a young man who succeeds by following the simple rules in a book.

Cast: 5 females, 12 males

Sets: 15

Choreographer: Bob Fosse

Score includes: "Happy to Keep His Dinner Warm," "I Believe In You," "How To Succeed," "Rosemary," "The Company Way," "Brotherhood of Man"

Orchestra: 5 Reeds (all double), 3 Trumpets, 3 Trombones, Horn, 2 Percussion, Guitar, Harp, and Strings

Cast Album: RCA Victor (Robert Morse, Rudy Vallee, Bonnie Scott, Charles Nelson Reilly, Ruth Kobart, Virginia Martin)

I Can Get It for You Wholesale (1962) (TW)

Music and lyrics by Harold Rome

Book by Jerome Weidman, based on Mr. Weidman's novel

Time: The 1930s

Plot: Concerns an overly ambitious young man who attempts by any possible means to become the head of a wholesale clothing concern.

Cast: 10 females, 14 males

Choreographer: Herbert Ross

Score includes: "I'm Not a Well Man," "When Gemini Meets Capricorn," "Momma, Momma," "The Sound of Money," "Have I Told You Lately?" "Miss Marmelstein," "Eat a Little Something"

Original Cast Album: Columbia (Barbra Streisand, Elliott Gould, Jack Kruschen, Marilyn Cooper, Lillian Roth, Sheree North, Harold Lang)

I Do! I Do! (1966) (MTI)

Music by Harvey Schmidt

Book and lyrics by Tom Jones, based on *The Fourposter* by Jan de Hartog

Time: Beginning just before the turn of the century and extending 50 years

Plot: Concerns a marriage and follows the couple through most of their lives.

Cast: 1 female, 1 male

Sets: 1 basic set with changes of furniture, etc.

Choreographer: Gower Champion

Score includes: "Together Forever," "Nobody's Perfect," "I Do, I Do," "All the Dearly Beloved," "My Cup Runneth Over," "What Is a Woman?"

Orchestra: 4 Reeds (doubles, but no Sax), 2 Trumpets, Trombone, 2 Horns, 2 Percussion, 2 Piano, Harp, and Strings

Original Cast Album: RCA Victor (Mary Martin, Robert Preston)

Illya Darling (1967) (TW)

Music by Manos Hadjidakis

Lyrics by Joe Darion

Book by Jules Dassin, based on the film *Never on Sunday*

Time: Set in Greece in the present

Plot: Concerns a charming prostitute and her love.

Cast: 6 females, 17 males

Sets: 13

Score includes: "Piraeus, My Love," "Golden Land," "Birthday Song," "Illya Darling," "Never on Sunday"

Cast Album: United Artists (Melina Mercouri, Titos Vandis, Nikos Kourkoulos, Orson Bean, Despo, Hal Linden)

I Married an Angel (1938) (R&H)

Music by Richard Rodgers

Lyrics by Lorenz Hart

Book by Rodgers and Hart, adapted by Lou Jacoby

Time: The present

Plot: A banker declares he will only marry an angel when suddenly a lovely one flies in. The trouble with her is that she tells only the truth—something that causes lots of trouble.

Cast: 17 females, 9 males

Sets: 8

Score includes: "Did You Ever Get Stung?," "I Married an Angel," "Spring Is Here," "I'll Tell The Man In The Street"

166

Irene (1973 revival) (TW)

Music by Harry Tierney

Lyrics by Joseph McCarthy

Additional music and lyrics by Charles Gaynor and Otis Clement

Book by Hugh Wheeler and Joseph Stein, from an adaptation by Harry Rigby, based on the play by James Montgomery

Time: The 1920s

Plot: A young piano-tuner (female) falls in love with a wealthy young socialite.

Cast: 6 females, 5 males

Sets: 8

Choreographer: Peter Gennaro

Score includes: "Alice Blue Gown," "An Irish Girl," "They Go Wild Over Me," "I'm Always Chasing Rainbows," "You Made Me Love You"

Orchestra: 5 Reeds (all double), 4 Trumpets, 3 Trombones, 2 Percussion, Harp, Guitar-Banjo, Organ-Piano, and Strings.

(1973 Revival) Cast Album: Columbia (Debbie Reynolds, George S. Irving, Patsy Kelly, Carmen Alvarez, Ruth Warwick)

Irma la Douce (1960) (TW)

Music by Marguerite Monnot

Book and lyrics by Alexandre Breffort (French); English book and lyrics by Julian More, David Heneker, and Monty Norman

Plot: Concerns a charming prostitute who falls in love with a law student, and the latter's jealousy. He disguises himself as a wealthy older man, grows tired of his double life, and "murders" his assumed character. He is found guilty of murder and imprisoned on Devil's Island. Hearing that he is to become a father, he escapes and arrives back in time to celebrate the baby's birth.

Cast: 1 female, 15 males

Sets: 2

Choreographer: Onna White

Score includes: "Dis-Donc," "The Bridge of Caulaincourt," "Our Language of Love," "From a Prison Cell"

Original Cast Album: Columbia (Elizabeth Seal, Clive Revill, Keith Michell)

It's a Bird, It's a Plane, It's Superman (1966) (TW)

Music by Charles Strouse

Lyrics by Lee Adams

Book by David Newman and Robert Benton, based on the comic strip

Plot: "A testament to the harrowing perplexities of 20th century man . . ." (the authors). It is a satire.

Cast: 11 females, 15 males

Sets: 12

Score includes: "We Need Him," "We Don't Matter at All," "Revenge," "You've Got Possibilities," "What I've Always Wanted," "Ooh, Do You Love You!"

Original Cast Album: Columbia (Bob Holiday, Jack Cassidy, Patricia Marand, Linda Lavin, Don Chastain, Michael O'Sullivan)

Jacques Brel Is Alive and Well and Living in Paris (1968) (MTI)

Music and lyrics by Jacques Brel; English lyrics and additional material by Eric Blau and Mort Shuman

Plot: This is a revue containing 25 Brel songs.

Cast: 2 females, 2 males

Sets: None

Score includes: "Marathon," "Timid Frieda," "Amsterdam," "Old Folks," "Carousel," "Fannette"

Orchestra: Piano-Celeste, Electric Guitar, Bass (Electric), Percussion, Piano

Original Cast Album: Columbia (Shawn Elliott, Mort Shuman, Elly Stone, Alice Whitfield)

Jesus Christ Superstar (1971) (MTI)

Music by Andrew Lloyd Webber

Lyrics by Tim Rice

Book based on the Passion of Christ

Time: The period leading up to the Crucifixion of Christ

Plot: As above.

Cast: 14

Sets: 1 basic set

Score includes: "Heaven on Their Minds," "Everything's Alright," "Hosanna," "I Don't Know How to Love Him," "This Jesus Must Die," "Pilate's Dream," "Gethsemane"

Orchestra: (Rock) Electric Guitar/Acoustic Guitar, Electric Bass Guitar, Piano/Organ, Drums/Percussion, Trumpet, Trombone, Horn, Flute/Piccolo, Flute/Clarinet, Oboe, Bassoon, Strings

Original (American) Cast Album: Decca (Ben Vereen, Jeff Fenholt, Yvonne Elliman, Bob Bingham, Denis Buckley, Barry Denner, Michael Jason)

Johnny Johnson (1936) (SF)

Music by Kurt Weill

Book and lyrics by Paul Green

Plot: Tender and comic satire dealing with the problems a young man faces dealing with the vicissitudes of war and peace.

Cast: 7 females, 27 males

Sets: 17

Score includes: "Listen to My Song," "Mon Ami, My Friend," "Oh, The Rio Grande," "Oh, Heart of Love"

Studio Recording: Heliodor (Burgess Meredith, Lotte Lenya, Hiram Sherman, Jane Connell)

The King and I (1951) (R&H)

Music by Richard Rodgers

Book and lyrics by Oscar Hammerstein II, based on *Anna and the King of Siam* by Margaret Landon

Time: 1860 (Siam)

Plot: Tells of a king's struggle to change himself and his people and of the Western school teacher who inspired him.

Cast: 4 females, 9 males

Sets: 9

Choreographer: Jerome Robbins

Score includes: "Getting To Know You," "We Kiss in a Shadow," "Shall We Dance?," "Something Wonderful," "Hello, Young Lovers," "I Whistle A Happy Tune"

Orchestra: 10 Strings, 7 Reeds, 3 Trumpets, 3 Horns, 2 Trombones, Tuba, Bass, Percussion

Original Cast Album: Decca (Yul Brynner, Gertrude Lawrence, Doretta Morrow, Dorothy Sarnoff)

Studio Recording: Columbia (Barbara Cook, Theodore Bikel, Jeanette Scovotti, Anita Darien)

Kismet (1953) (MTI)

Musical adaptation and lyrics by Robert Wright and George Forrest, based on themes by Alexander Borodin

Book by Charles Lederer and Luther Davis, based on a play by Edmund Knoblock

Time: Oriental never-never land—story-book

Plot: Deals with a roguish poet-beggar, his daughter's romance with the Caliph, and his own marriage with the Wazir's wife.

Cast: 13 females, 24 males

Score includes: "Fate," "Baubles, Bangles, and Beads," "Stranger in Paradise," "And This Is My Beloved"

Orchestra: 6 Reeds (no Sax), 3 Trumpets, 1 Horn, 2 Trombones, 1 Tuba, Harp, Percussion, and Strings

Original Cast Album: Columbia (Alfred Drake, Doretta Morrow, Joan Diener, Richard Kiley)

Kiss Me, Kate (1948) (TW)

Music and lyrics by Cole Porter

Book by Bella and Sam Spewack, based in part on Shakespeare's *The Taming of the Shrew*

Time: Contemporary and Shakespearean costumes

Cast: 3 females, 11 males

Sets: 12

Choreographer: Hanya Holm

Score includes: "Another Op'nin', Another Show," "Why Can't You Behave?," "Wunderbar," "So in Love," "I Hate Men," "Too Darn Hot," "Always True To You in My Fashion"

Orchestra: 5 Reeds (doubling Saxophones), 1 Horn, 3 Trumpets, 1 Trombone, Harp, Piano-Celeste, Guitar-Mandolin (doubles Violin)

Original Cast Album: Columbia (Alfred Drake, Lisa Kirk, Patricia Morison, Harold Lang, Harry Clark)

Knickerbocker Holiday (1938) (R&H)

Music by Kurt Weill

Book and lyrics by Maxwell Anderson, suggested by Washington Irving's *Father Knickerbocker's History*

Time: 1647

Plot: Politics and romance in the growing New World.

Cast: 2 females, 14 males

Sets: 3

Score includes: "September Song," "It Never Was You," "Young People Think About Love," "How Can You Tell an American?"

Lady in the Dark (1941) (TW)

Music by Kurt Weill

Lyrics by Ira Gershwin

Book by Moss Hart

Time: The present and fantastic "flashbacks"

Plot: A lady editor of a fashion magazine can't make up her mind. Alternate scenes are played in a psychiatrist's office. Each of these is a fantastic "operetta" in which the lady's life is played with different accents and imaginings.

Cast: 11 females, 9 males

Sets: 2

Score includes: "One Life To Live," "Girl of the Moment," "This Is New," "The Princess of Pure Delight," "The Saga of Jenny," "My Ship"

Studio Record Album: Columbia (Risë Stevens, Adolph Green, John Reardon)

Li'l Abner (1956) (TW)

Music by Gene de Paul

Lyrics by Johnny Mercer

Book by Norman Panana and Melvin Frank, based on the comic strip by Al Capp

Time: The present in fantastic rural America

Plot: Dogpatch, the scene of the show, has been declared unnecessary—Congress has agreed to relocate the citizens and use the area for atomic tests. There is much romance, particularly between Daisy Mae and Li'l Abner.

Cast: 8 females, 15 males

Sets: 11

Choreographer: Michael Kidd

Score includes: "A Typical Day," "If I Had My Druthers," "Jubilation T. Cornpone," "Namely You," "The Country's in the Very Best of Hands," "Progress"

Orchestra: 5 Reeds (doubling Sax), 3 Trumpets, 3 Trombones, Percussion, Banjo-Guitar, Piano, and Strings

Original Cast Album: Columbia (Stubby Kaye, Edie Adams, Julie Newmar, Tina Louise, Peter Palmer)

Little Mary Sunshine (1959) (SF)

Music, lyrics, and book by Rick Besoyan

Time: Early in the present century, high in the Rocky Mountains

Plot: A spoof of the operettas of the twenties, *Rose Marie* in particular.

Cast: 8 females, 11 males

Sets: 6

Score includes: "Little Mary Sunshine," "Look for a Sky of Blue," "Once in a Blue Moon," "Every Little Nothing," "Naughty, Naughty Nancy," "Colorado Love Call"

Orchestra: Small combo

Original Cast Album: Capitol (Eileen Brennan, John McMartin, Elizabeth Parrish, William Graham, Mario Siletti)

Little Me (1962) (TW)

Music by Cy Coleman

Lyrics by Carolyn Leigh

Book by Neil Simon, based on a novel by Patrick Dennis

Time: Past and present

Plot: Concerns a no-talent actress whose aim is to acquire wealth, culture, and social position.

172

Cast: 8 females, 15 males

Score includes: "The Other Side of the Tracks," "I've Got Your Number," "Dimples," "Real Live Girl," "Little Me"

Original Cast Album: RCA Victor (Nancy Andrews, Virginia Martin, Sid Caesar, Joey Faye, Mort Marshall)

A Little Night Music (1973) (MTI)

Music and lyrics by Stephen Sondheim

Book by Hugh Wheeler, suggested by an Ingmar Bergman film

Time: Turn-of-the-century Sweden

Plot: Mismatched love that becomes straightened out in the end.

Cast: 8 females, 5 males

Sets: 2 basic sets with "slides" that define places

Score includes: "Now," "Later," "Soon," "Remember?," "You Must Meet My Wife," "Liaisons," "Every Day a Little Death," "A Weekend in the Country," "Send in the Clowns," "The Miller's Son"

Orchestra: 5 Reeds (all double, but no Sax), 3 Horns, 2 Trumpets, 1 Trombone, 1 Percussion, Harp, Piano-Celeste, and Strings

Original Cast Album: Columbia (Hermione Gingold, Mark Lambert, Victoria Mallory, Len Cariou, Glynis Johns, Laurence Guittard, Patricia Elliott, D. Jamin Bartlett)

Lorelei (1974) (TW)

Music by Jule Styne

Lyrics by Betty Comden and Adolph Green

Book by Kenny Solms and Gail Parent, based on the musical *Gentlemen Prefer Blondes,* with book by Anita Loos and Joseph Fields, adapted from Miss Loos' novel *Gentlemen Prefer Blondes*

Time: 1920s and the present

Plot: Lorelei Lee looking back on her 1920s escapades from the viewpoint of the present.

Cast: 8 females, 14 males

Sets: 9

Score includes: "Looking Back," "Bye, Bye Baby," "A Little Girl from Little Rock," "You Say You Care," "Diamonds Are a Girl's Best Friend"

Orchestra: 5 Reeds (doubling Sax), 2 Horns, 3 Trumpets, 2 Trombones, Percussion, Guitar-Banjo, Piano-Celeste, and Strings

Original Cast Album: MGM-Verve (Carol Channing, Lee Roy Reams, Dody Goodman, Peter Palmer)

Lost in the Stars (1949) (R&H)

Music by Kurt Weill

Book and lyrics by Maxwell Anderson, based on Alan Paton's novel *Cry, the Beloved Country*

Time: The present in South Africa

Plot: The tragic results of a divided black and white society.

Cast: 8 females, 23 males, mostly black; chorus acts largely as a Greek chorus

Sets: 20

Score includes: "Cry, the Beloved Country," "Thousands of Miles," "The Little Gray House," "Lost In The Stars"

Orchestra: 3 Reeds (including Sax), 1 Trumpet, Harp, Percussion, Piano-Accordian, 2 Violins, 2 Celli, 1 Bass

Original Cast Album: Decca (Todd Duncan, Lavern French, Mabel Hart, Warren Coleman, Georgette Harvey, William Marshall, Inez Matthews)

Lovely Ladies, Kind Gentlemen (1970) (SF)

Music and lyrics by Stan Freeman and Franklin Underwood

Book by John Patrick, based on Mr. Patrick's play *Teahouse of the August Moon* and the novel by Vern J. Sneider

Time: Post-World War II in Okinawa (1946)

Cast: 3 females, 20 males

Score includes: "One Side of the World," "This Time," "Simple Word," "Call Me Back"

Maggie Flynn (1968) (SF)

Music, lyrics, and book by Hugo Peretti, Luigi Creatore, and George Weiss, based on an idea by John Flaxman

Time: 1863

Plot: Maggie runs an asylum for black children orphaned by the Civil War. She is about to marry a Union officer when her husband, who left her eight years before, returns as a circus clown. Love wins out.

Cast: 15 females, 27 males

Sets: 15

Score includes: "Never Gonna Make Me Fight," "Learn How to Laugh," "Maggie Flynn," "I Won't Let It Happen Again," "Why Can't I Walk Away?"

Original Cast Album: RCA Victor (Shirley Jones, Jack Cassidy, Robert Kaye, Sybil Bowan, William James)

Mame (1966) (TW)

Music and lyrics by Jerry Herman

Book by Jerome Lawrence and Robert E. Lee, based on their play *Auntie Mame* and the novel by Patrick Dennis

Time: The twenties

Plot: Mame is a well-to-do New Yorker who is surprised by the arrival of an orphaned nephew. The show concerns the peccadilloes of aunt and nephew, Patrick.

Cast: 10 females, 16 males

Sets: 10

Choreographer: Onna White

Score includes: "My Best Girl," "Mame," "Bosom Buddies," "Gooch's Song," "It's Today," "Open A New Window," "If He Walked into My Life"

Orchestra: 5 Reeds (with Sax), 2 Trumpets, 3 Trombones, Percussion, Harp, Guitar-Banjo, Piano-Celeste, and Strings

Cast Album: Columbia (Angela Lansbury, Beatrice Arthur, Jane Connell, Charles Braswell, Jerry Lanning)

Man of La Mancha (1965) (TW)

Music by Mitch Leigh

Lyrics by Joe Darion

Book by Dale Wasserman, based on *Don Quixote* by Miguel de Cervantes

Time: Spain at the end of the 16th century

Cast: 5 females, 21 males

Set: Common room of a stone prison vault—a basic set. Guards enter and exit by means of a long flight of stairs that descends from

175

above to the prison. Various places are suggested by small pieces of scenery.

Choreographer: Jack Cole

Score includes: "Dulcinea," "I Really Like Him," "The Quest (The Impossible Dream)," "Aldonza," "To Each His Dulcinea"

Orchestra: (divided in two parts, playing on each side of the backstage area) 5 Reeds (no Sax), 2 Horns, 2 Trumpets, 2 Trombones, 2 Spanish Guitars, 3 Percussion, String Bass

Original Cast Recording: RCA Victor (Isabel Bigley, Ray Walston, Bill Diener, Robert Rounseville, Ray Middleton, Eleanor Knapp)

Me and Juliet (1953) (R&H)

Music by Richard Rodgers

Book and lyrics by Oscar Hammerstein II

Time: The present, in a theater

Plot: A play within a play—backstage tale of love and jealousy.

Cast: 15 females, 16 males

Sets: 13

Score includes: "No Other Love," "Keep It Gay," "It's Me, "It Feels Good," "Marriage Type Love"

Original Cast Recording: RCA Victor (Isabel Bigley, Ray Walston, Bill Hayes, Joan McCracken)

The Me Nobody Knows (1970) (SF)

Music by Gary William Friedman

Lyrics by Will Holt

Adapted by Robert H. Livingston and Herb Schapiro from *The Me Nobody Knows*, a compendium of children's writings by S. M. Joseph

Time: Present, in a big city ghetto

Plot: There is no specific plot; the evening consists of poems, and songs made from poems, relating largely to ghetto life.

Cast: 6 females, 6 males (young teenagers)

Choreographer: Patricia Birch

Score includes: "Fugue for Four Girls," "Rejoice," "War Babies," "Dream Babies," "Something Beautiful"

Original Cast Album: Atlantic Records (Gerri Dean, Kevin Lindsay, Laura Michaels, Hattie Winston, Jose Fernandez)

The Most Happy Fella (1956) (MTI)

Music, lyrics, and libretto by Frank Loesser, based on Sidney Howard's play *They Knew What They Wanted*

Time: The present, rural

Plot: An aging Italian-American with an inferiority complex writes to a waitress, inviting her to write him at his Napa Valley ranch. He sends her the photograph of his handsome young foreman, claiming it is a photograph of himself. The waitress agrees to marry Tony, Tony's car overturns, and the girl mistakes the foreman (Joey) for Tony. Complications ensue, but everything turns out happily.

Cast: 9 females, 16 males

Sets: 7

Score includes: "Joey, Joey, Joey," "Big D," "Standing on the Corner," "Rosabella," "Abbondanza," "My Heart Is So Full of You"

Orchestra: 5 Reeds (only the 3rd doubles as Sax), 3 Trumpets, 2 Trombones, Harp, Percussion, Guitar, and Strings

Original Cast Album: Columbia (Susan Johnson, Robert Weede, Mona Paulee, Jo Sullivan, Art Lund)

Mr. President (1962) (MTI)

Music and lyrics by Irving Berlin

Book by Howard Lindsay and Russel Crouse

Time: The present

Plot: Concerns a U.S. President and his family life together with his official duties.

Cast: 6 females, 17 males

Sets: Various parts of the White House and four other locales.

Score includes: "Let's Go Back To The Waltz," "In Our Hideaway," "Empty Pockets Filled with Love," "Is He the Only Man in the World?"

Orchestra: 4 Reeds (including Sax), 3 Trumpets, 2 Trombones, Harp, Percussion, Guitar, and Strings

Original Cast Album: Columbia (David Brooks, Robert Ryan, Nanette Fabray, Anita Gillette, Jack Washburn, Stanley Grover)

Mr. Wonderful (1956) (MTI)

Music and lyrics by Jerry Bock, Larry Holofcener, and George Weiss

Book by Joseph Stein and Will Glickman

Time: The present

Plot: A promising nightclub entertainer prefers to remain a small-town performer. His friends stake their life savings on his big-time debut. At the last minute, he backs out and his friends leave him. He is given a second chance, makes good, regains his lost friendships and his girl.

Cast: 11 females, 14 males

Sets: 9

Score includes: "Mr. Wonderful," "Without You I'm Nothing," "Talk To Him," "Too Close for Comfort"

Original Cast Album: Decca (Sammy Davis, Jr., Chita Rivèra, Jack Carter, Olga James)

The Music Man (1957) (MTI)

Music, lyrics, and book by Meredith Willson

Story by Meredith Willson and Franklin Lacey

Time: 1912

Plot: Concerns a charming if dishonest traveling salesman who sells musical instruments, his effect (for good) on the people of a small Iowa town, and his romance with the local librarian.

Cast: 10 females, 8 males

Sets: 13

Choreographer: Onna White

Score includes: "Trouble," "Goodnight, My Someone," "Seventy-Six Trombones," "My White Knight," "Pick-a-Little, Talk-a-Little," "Till There Was You"

Orchestra: (Broadway version) 5 Reeds, 3 Trumpets, 3 Trombones, Percussion, Piano, and Strings (a reduced version is available)

Original Cast Album: Capitol (Robert Preston, David Burns, Iggie Wolfington, Barbara Cook, Pert Kelton, Eddie Hodges)

My Fair Lady (1956) (TW)

Music by Frederick Loewe

Book and lyrics by Alan Jay Lerner, adapted from George Bernard Shaw's *Pygmalion* and Gabriel Pascal's film

Time: London, 1912

Plot: Deals with an egocentric speech teacher who transforms an ignorant flower girl into a lady and the problems that arise afterward.

Cast: 8 females, 17 males

Sets: 11

Choreographer: Hanya Holm

Score includes: "Why Can't The English?," "Wouldn't It Be Loverly?," "With A Little Bit Of Luck," "I'm An Ordinary Man," "Just You Wait," "The Rain In Spain," "I Could Have Danced All Night," "On The Street Where You Live"

Orchestra: 5 Reeds (all legitimate), 2 Horns, 3 Trumpets, 2 Trombones, Tuba, Percussion, Harp, and Strings (the show is also scored for reduced combo, band, and for 2 pianos)

Original Cast Album: Columbia (Julie Andrews, Rex Harrison, Robert Coote, Stanley Holloway)

New Girl in Town (1957) (MTI)

Music and lyrics by Bob Merrill

Book by George Abbott, based on Eugene O'Neill's play *Anna Christie*

Time: Early in the present century

Plot: A tugboat operator has not seen his daughter Anna in many years. It is clear when she arrives that she is a hard woman of the world. In the course of the play, Anna reforms and is readily accepted by her father's friends. She also falls in love.

Cast: 13 females, 16 males

Choreographer: Bob Fosse

Score includes: "On The Farm," "Flings," "It's Good To Be Alive," "Did You Choose Your Eyes?," "Sunshine Girl," "Look at 'Er"

Original Cast Album: RCA Victor (Gwen Verdon, Cameron Prud'homme, George Wallace, Thelma Ritter)

No Strings (1962) (R&H)

Music and lyrics by Richard Rodgers

Book by Samuel Taylor

Time: Present

Plot: An expatriate American novelist and a black jet-setting, high-fashion model have a complex love affair.

Cast: 5 females, 5 males

Sets: 5

Choreographer: Joe Layton

Score includes: "The Sweetest Sounds," "No Strings," "Look No Further," "Love Makes The World Go," "Nobody Told Me"

Orchestra: As the title indicates, the orchestra contains no strings. As written, the orchestra is situated backstage, and occasionally on stage.

Original Cast Album: Capitol (Diahann Carroll, Richard Kiley, Bernice Massi)

No, No, Nanette (1971 revival) (TW)

Music by Vincent Youmans

Lyrics by Irving Caesar and Otto Harbach

Book by Otto Harbach and Frank Mandel, adapted by Burt Shevelove

Time: 1925

Plot: The story of Jimmy Smith and all the trouble he gets into and out of on a weekend in New York and Atlantic City.

Cast: 7 females, 3 males

Sets: 3 (this musical is in 3 acts)

Score includes: "Tea For Two," "I Want to Be Happy," "Too Many Rings Around Rosie," "You Can Dance with Any Girl At All"

Orchestra: 5 Reeds (with Sax), 1 Horn, 3 Trumpets, 2 Trombones, Percussion, Guitar, Banjo, Ukelele, and Strings

(1971 Revival) Cast Album: Columbia (Patsy Kelly, Helen Gallagher, Ruby Keeler, Jack Gilford, Bobby Van, Susan Watson)

Oklahoma! (1943) (R&H)

Music by Richard Rodgers

Book and lyrics by Oscar Hammerstein II, based on Lynn Riggs' play *Green Grow the Lilacs*

Time: Indian Territory about the turn of the century

Plot: Two girls and two boys in love get sidetracked for a time. The complications end happily.

Cast: 4 females, 7 males

Sets: 6

Choreographer: Agnes deMille

Score includes: "Oh, What a Beautiful Mornin'," "The Surrey with the Fringe on Top," "Many a New Day," "People Will Say We're in Love," "Lonely Room"

Original Cast Album: Decca (Alfred Drake, Joan Roberts, Celeste Holm)

Film Soundtrack: Capitol (Gordon MacRae, Shirley Jones)

Oliver! (1965) (TW)

Music, lyrics, and book by Lionel Bart, based on Charles Dickens' *Oliver Twist*

Time: About 1850, London

Plot: Oliver, a young boy, is "sold" by the head of a workhouse where he lives to an undertaker. He runs away and is picked up by another boy, the Artful Dodger, who works for Fagin. The latter keeps many other boys who work as pickpockets. Oliver is found by his own grandfather, has adventures with Bill Sikes, a hardened criminal, and his mistress Nancy. Melodrama, love, and pathos.

Cast: 6 females, 10 males (several young boys)

Sets: 8

Score includes: "Where Is Love?," "Consider Yourself," "I'd Do Anything," "You've Got to Pick a Pocket or Two," "It's a Fine Life," "Who Will Buy?," "As Long As He Needs Me"

Orchestra: 4 Reeds (no Sax), 2 Horns, 2 Trumpets, 2 Trombones, 2 Percussion, Piano, and Strings (also available with reduced instrumentation)

Original Cast Album: RCA Victor (Clive Revill, David Jones, Georgia Brown, Danny Sewell, Bruce Prochnik)

On a Clear Day You Can See Forever (1965) (TW)

Music by Burton Lane

Book and lyrics by Alan Jay Lerner

Time: The present and the 18th century

Plot: A handsome psychiatrist is intrigued by a young woman who is so acutely clairvoyant that, under hypnosis, she can recall the details of her previous 18th-century existence, including a love affair.

Cast: 7 females, 14 males

Sets: 5

Score includes: "On a Clear Day," "Hurry, It's Lovely Up Here," "What Did I Have That I Don't Have?," "On the S.S. Bernard Cohn," "Come Back to Me"

Original Cast Album: RCA Victor (John Cullum, Barbara Harris, William Daniels, Clifford David)

On the Town (1944) (TW)

Music by Leonard Bernstein

Book and lyrics by Betty Comden and Adolph Green, based on an idea by Jerome Robbins

Plot: 3 young sailors on a holiday in New York.

Cast: 11 females, 16 males

Sets: 15

Choreographer: Jerome Robbins

Score includes: "New York, New York," "Carried Away," "Lonely Town," "Lucky To Be Me," "Some Other Time"

Studio Cast Album: Columbia (Nancy Walker, Betty Comden, Adolph Green, John Reardon)

Once Upon a Mattress (1959) (MTI)

Music by Mary Rodgers

Lyrics by Marshall Barer

Book by Jay Thompson, Marshall Barer, and Dean Fuller

Time: "Many Moons Ago"—quasi-medieval

Plot: Based loosely on the fairy tale "The Princess And The Pea."

Cast: 14 females, 15 males

Sets: 13

Score includes: "Shy," "Sensitivity," "In A Little While," "Happily Ever After," "Yesterday I Loved You"

Orchestra: 4 Reeds (no Sax), 1 Horn, 3 Trumpets, 3 Trombones, Percussion, Harp, Guitar, and Strings

Original Cast Album: Kapp (Harry Snow, Joe Bova, Jane White, Matt Mattox, Carol Burnett, Anne Jones, Allen Case)

110 in the Shade (1963) (TW)

Music by Harvey Schmidt

Lyrics by Tom Jones

Book by N. Richard Nash, based on his play *The Rainmaker*

Time: The present in a Western state

Plot: A family of men try unsuccessfully to marry off the spinster daughter. An itinerant con man, posing as a rainmaker, persuades her to think of herself as a real woman—every woman is beautiful! There are complications but the rainmaker finally makes it rain, and leaves the girl to receive the sheriff as a suitor.

Cast: 4 females, 16 males

Sets: 9

Choreographer: Agnes deMille

Score includes: "Lizzie's Comin' Home," "Love, Don't Turn Away," "Rain Song," "A Man and A Woman," "Everything Beautiful Happens At Night," "Melisande," "Is It Really Me?"

Orchestra: 6 Reeds (only 1 Sax), 2 Horns, 3 Trumpets, 1 Trombone, 2 Percussion, Guitar, Harp, and Strings

Original Cast Album: RCA Victor (Stephen Douglass, Will Geer, Inga Swenson, Robert Horton)

One Touch of Venus (1943) (TW)

Music by Kurt Weill

Lyrics by Ogden Nash

Book by S.J. Perelman and Ogden Nash

Plot: A statue of Venus is discovered. A young barber, admiring the statue, places the engagement ring intended for his fiancée on her finger and she comes to life.

Cast: 6 females, 12 males

Sets: 9

Choreographer: Agnes deMille

Score includes: "One Touch of Venus," "West Wind," "How Much I Love You," "Speak Low," "That's Him"

Original Cast Album: Decca (John Boles, Paula Lawrence, Teddy Hart, Harry Clark, Kenny Baker, Mary Martin)

Out of This World (1950) (TW)

Music and lyrics by Cole Porter

Book by Dwight Taylor and Reginald Lawrence

Time: Modern-day Greece

Plot: Based loosely on the Amphitryon legend. Jupiter falls in love with a beautiful human newlywed and descends to earth to make love to her. Juno, his wife, follows, and becomes involved with comic gangsters. The gods eventually return to Olympus, happily, leaving the mortal woman to readjust to a humdrum life.

Cast: 5 females, 6 males

Sets: 10

Score includes: "I Jupiter, I Rex," "Use Your Imagination," "Where, Oh Where," "I Am Loved," "They Couldn't Compare to You," "Nobody's Chasing Me," "Cherry Pies Ought to Be You"

Original Cast Album: Columbia (William Redfield, George Jongeyans, Priscilla Gillette, William Eythe, Charlotte Greenwood, Barbara Ashley, David Burns)

Paint Your Wagon (1951) (TW)

Music by Frederick Loewe

Book and lyrics by Alan Jay Lerner

Time: 1853, northern California

Plot: Gold is found on the land of Ben Rumson, and his land soon becomes a thriving mining town. His daughter falls in love with a young miner, but Ben sends her off to school. The gold runs out, and the daughter returns home and resumes her romance.

Cast: 7 females, 22 males

Sets: 9

Score includes: "I'm On My Way," "I Talk to the Trees," "They Call the Wind Maria," "How Can I Wait?," "Another Autumn"

Cast Album: RCA Victor (James Barton, Olga San Juan, Kay Medford, Tony Bavaar)

The Pajama Game (1954) (MTI)

Music and lyrics by Richard Adler and Jerry Ross

Book by George Abbott and Richard Bissell, based on Bissell's novel *7½ Cents*

Time: The present

Plot: A new foreman has just been hired at a pajama factory. Unknowingly, he runs into a dispute between the management and the workers. The latter are represented by the heroine, their union steward. Romance is split up and, when the union wins its raise, romance is restored.

Cast: 5 females, 12 males

Sets: Sketchy depictions of various offices and hallways (and a full stage sewing room) in the factory, plus a kitchen, a nightclub, and a picnic area.

Choreographer: Bob Fosse

Score includes: "A New Town Is a Blue Town," "I'm Not At All in Love," "I'll Never Be Jealous Again," "Hey There," "There Once Was a Man," "Steam Heat," "Hernando's Hideaway"

Orchestra: 5 Reeds (including Sax), 3 Trumpets, 3 Trombones, Guitar, Percussion, Piano, and Strings

Original Cast Album: Columbia (Eddie Foy, Jr., Carol Haney, John Raitt, Reta Shaw, Janis Paige)

Pal Joey (1940) (R&H)

Music by Richard Rodgers
Lyrics by Lorenz Hart
Book by John O'Hara

Time: The present

Plot: A wealthy and socially prominent married woman falls for an untalented young punk. She "keeps" him, creates a nightclub for him, and enjoys life until two shady characters threaten blackmail and she leaves Joey as she found him.

Cast: 8 females, 12 males

Sets: 8

Choreographer: Robert Alton

Score includes: "I Could Write a Book," "Bewitched, Bothered and Bewildered," "In Our Little Den of Iniquity," "Zip"

Studio Cast Album: Columbia (Vivienne Segal, Harold Lang)

Peter Pan (1954) (SF)

Music by Mark Charlap, additional music by Jule Styne

Lyrics by Carolyn Leigh, additional lyrics by Betty Comden and Adolph Green

Book by J.M. Barrie

Time: Past and Never-never land

Plot: The familiar story of Peter Pan taking the Darling children to Never-never-land, encountering pirates, and so on.

Cast: 8 females, 19 males

Sets: 7

Choreographer: Jerome Robbins

Score includes: "I've Got to Crow," "Neverland," "Pirate Song," "Wendy," "I Won't Grow Up"

Original Cast Album: Columbia (Kathy Nolan, Margalo Gillmore, Cyril Ritchard, Mary Martin)

Pippin (1972) (MTI)

Music and lyrics by Stephen Schwartz

Book by Roger O. Hirson

Time: 8th-century France

Plot: The dilemma of Pippin, the son of Charlemagne, who seeks fulfillment on his own.

Cast: 4 females, 10 males

Sets: Unit set with smaller pieces set on sliders (performed with no intermission)

Choreographer: Bob Fosse

Score includes: "Corner of the Sky," "Glory," "With You," "Spread a Little Sunshine," "Extraordinary"

Orchestra: 2 Reeds (no Sax), 1 Horn, 1 Trumpet, 2 Trombones, Guitar, Percussion, Piano I (doubling harpsichord), Piano II (doubling organ), Strings, Electric Bass

Original Cast Album: Motown (Ben Vereen, John Rubenstein, Leland Palmer, Irene Ryan, Jill Clayburgh)

Plain and Fancy (1955) (SF)

Music by Albert Hague

Lyrics by Arnold B. Horwitt

Book by Joseph Stein and Will Glickman

Time: Present-day rural America (Amish country)

Plot: Romantic complications involving worldly wise New Yorkers among the Amish.

Cast: 11 females, 18 males

Sets: 13

Score includes: "It Wonders Me," "Young and Foolish," "This Is All Very New to Me," "Follow Your Heart"

Original Cast Album: Capitol (Shirl Conway, Richard Derr, Gloria Marlowe, Stefan Schnabel, Nancy Andrews, Barbara Cook, David Daniels)

Promises, Promises (1968) (TW)

Music by Burt Bacharach

Lyrics by Hal David

Book by Neil Simon, based on the film *The Apartment* by Billy Wilder and I.A.L. Diamond

Time: The present

Plot: An ambitious but shy young man lends his apartment for extra-marital purposes to various officials and friends in his office. The effects on his own life are nearly disastrous.

187

Cast: 10 females, 13 males

Sets: 11

Choreographer: Michael Bennett

Score includes: "I'll Never Fall in Love Again," "Promises, Promises," "She Likes Basketball," "Knowing When to Leave," "Whoever You Are," "Wanting Things"

Orchestra: 4 Reeds (including Sax), 1 Horn, 3 Trumpets, 2 Trombones, 2 Guitars (II doubles bass guitar), Electric Piano, 2 Percussion, Strings (the orchestra can be played minus 1 Trombone and all Strings except bass; four voices are used in the orchestra pit)

Original Cast Album: United Artists (Jerry Orbach, Jill O'Hara, Marian Mercer, Edward Winter)

Purlie (1970) (SF)

Music by Gary Geld

Lyrics by Peter Udell

Book by Ossie Davis, Philip Rose, and Peter Udell, based on the play *Purlie Victorious* by Ossie Davis

Time: Present

Plot: Concerns a new-fangled preacher whose mission is to integrate whites with the blacks.

Cast: 4 females, 4 males

Sets: 5

Score includes: "Walk Him up the Stairs," "I Got Love," "New Fangled Preacher Man," "He Can Do It," "The World Is Comin' To A Start"

Original Cast Album: Ampex (Cleavon Little, Linda Hopkins, Melba Moore, Sherman Hemsley, John Heffernan)

Redhead (1959) (MTI)

Music by Albert Hague

Lyrics by Dorothy Fields

Book by Herbert and Dorothy Fields, Sidney Sheldon, and David Shaw

Time: Turn of the century

Plot: The search for Jack the Ripper. Mystery and romance in a waxworks.

188

Cast: 7 females, 8 males

Sets: 10

Choreographer: Bob Fosse

Score includes: "Just for Once," "Merely Marvelous," "I'll Try," "Look Who's in Love," "Pick-Pocket Tango"

Orchestra: 5 Reeds (including Sax), 3 Trumpets, 3 Trombones, 1 Horn, Percussion, Guitar, Harp, and Strings

Original Cast Album: RCA Victor (Gwen Verdon, Richard Kiley, Leonard Stone, Cynthia Latham, Bob Dixon)

Riverwind (1962) (MTI)

Music, lyrics, and book by John Jennings

Time: The present

Plot: A middle-aged couple revisit the scene of their honeymoon. A young girl is confronted by romance with a man of the world. A free-thinking couple solve their conflict with a conformist society.

Cast: 4 females, 3 males (no ensemble)

Score includes: "Riverwind," "Sew the Buttons On," "I Want a Surprise," "Pardon Me While I Dance"

Orchestra: Bass, Percussion, and Piano

Original Cast Album: London

The Roar of the Greasepaint—The Smell of the Crowd (1965) (TW)

Music, lyrics, and book by Leslie Bricusse and Anthony Newley

Time: Anytime

Plot: An allegory—a confrontation between the "haves" and the "have-nots."

Cast: 2 females, 4 males

Set: "A rocky place"

Score includes: "Who Can I Turn To?," "The Joker," "Where Would You Be Without Me?," "A Wonderful Day Like Today," "Feeling Good"

Original Cast Album: RCA Victor (Anthony Newley, Cyril Ritchard, Sally Smith, Joyce Jillson, Gilbert Price, Murray Tannenbaum)

The Robber Bridegroom (1976) (MTI)

Music by Robert Waldman

Book and lyrics by Alfred Uhry, based on the novella by Eudora Welty

Time: 200 years or so ago, in Mississippi

Plot: Jamie, the robber, saved the richest planter in the county from the Harp Gang. The planter's daughter made the moon sizzle one evening a while back. There is dancing, gaiety, confusion, and romance.

Cast: 6 females, 12 males

Sets: A unit set (played without intermission)

Score includes: "Once Upon the Notchey Trace," "Two Heads," "Deeper in the Woods," "Riches"

Orchestra: 3 Violins, Mandolin, 2 Guitars, Bass, and Banjo

Original Cast Album: OC (Barry Bostwick, Barbara Lang)

The Rothschilds (1970) (SF)

Music by Jerry Bock

Lyrics by Sheldon Harnick

Book by Sherman Yellen, based on *The Rothschilds* by Frederic Morton

Time: 19th century

Plot: An account of the Rothschild family, progressing from the ghetto to the stock exchanges and courts of Europe.

Cast: 4 females, 22 males

Choreographer: Michael Kidd

Score includes: "Pleasure and Privilege," "One Room," "Rothschild and Sons," "I'm in Love! I'm in Love!," "In My Own Lifetime"

Original Cast Album: Columbia (Keene Curtis, Paul Hecht, Hal Linden, Jill Clayburgh)

Say, Darling (1958) (TW)

Music by Jule Styne

Lyrics by Betty Comden and Adolph Green

Book by Richard Bissell, Abe Burrows, and Marian Bissell, based on Richard Bissell's novel

Time: The present

Plot: Bissell's recollections of his first time in New York from the middle west, working with Broadway types to adapt his book *7½ Cents* into the musical *The Pajama Game.*

Cast: 8 females, 20 males

Sets: 8

Score includes: "Try to Love Me Just As I Am," "It's Doom," "Say, Darling," "Dance Only With Me"

Original Cast Album: RCA Victor (David Wayne, Vivian Blaine, Johnny Desmond)

Seesaw (1973) (SF)

Music by Cy Coleman

Lyrics by Dorothy Fields

Book by Michael Bennett, based on the play *Two for the Seesaw* by William Gibson

Time: The present

Cast: 5 females, 3 males

Sets: 10

Choreographer: Michael Bennett

Score includes: "Seesaw," "Nobody Does It Like Me," "He's Good for Me," "You're a Lovable Lunatic," "You've Got It," "It's Not Where You Start"

Original Cast Album: Buddah (Ken Howard, Michelle Lee, Tommy Tune)

1776 (1969) (MTI)

Music and lyrics by Sherman Edwards

Book by Peter Stone, based on a concept by Sherman Edwards

Time: 1776

Plot: The events in the Continental Congress that nearly lead to the *non*signing of the Declaration of Independence.

Cast: 2 females, 24 males

Sets: 4 (performed without an intermission)

Score includes: "Momma, Look Sharp," "Till Then," "Is Anybody There?," "He Plays the Violin," "Molasses to Rum," "Lees of Old Virginia"

Orchestra: 4 Reeds (no Sax), Trumpet/Piccolo Trumpet, 2 Horns, 3 Trombones (third doubles Tuba), Percussion, and Strings

Original Cast Album: Columbia (William Daniels, Virginia Vestoff, Ronald Holgate, Paul Hecht, Scott Jarvis, Clifford David, Ken Howard)

70, Girls, 70 (1971) (SF)

Music by John Kander

Lyrics by Fred Ebb

Book by Fred Ebb and Norman L. Martin, adapted by Joe Masteroff, from the play *Breath of Spring* by Peter Coke

Time: The present

Plot: The older set decides to spice things up around the retirement home by becoming shoplifters.

Cast: 12 females, 11 males

Sets: 9

Score includes: "Old Folks," "The Caper," "You and I, Love," "Do We?," "Go Visit," "70, Girls, 70," "Yes"

Original Cast Album: Columbus (Mildred Natwick, Lillian Roth, Gilia Lamb, Hans Conried, Lillian Hayman, Goldye Shaw)

She Loves Me (1963) (TW)

Music by Jerry Bock

Lyrics by Sheldon Harnick

Book by Joe Masteroff, based on the play by Miklos Laszlo (the film *The Shop Around The Corner* was adapted from the same play as this musical)

Time: The 1930s (Budapest)

Plot: Employees of a perfume store and their relationships. The young manager corresponds with a "dear friend" whom he has never met. A young lady applies for a job; we discover it is she who is corresponding with the young manager. There are confusions, especially since the two seem antagonistic to each other. All ends happily.

Score includes: "Days Gone By," "A Trip to the Library," "I Don't Know His Name," "Will He Like Me?," "Dear Friend," "Ice Cream," "She Loves Me"

192

Original Cast Album: MGM (Ludwig Donath, Barbara Cook, Jack Cassidy, Daniel Massey, Nathaniel Frey, Barbara Baxley)

Show Boat (1927) (R&H)

Music by Jerome Kern

Book and lyrics by Oscar Hammerstein II, based on Edna Ferber's novel

Time: The 1890s to 1927

Plot: Romance between a young girl, daughter of the owner of a show boat, and a gambler. Choruses of blacks and whites.

Cast: 5 females, 4 males

Sets: 11

Score includes: "Ol' Man River," "Make Believe," "Why Do I Love You?," "You Are Love," "Can't Help Lovin' Dat Man," "Bill"

First Film Soundtrack: Columbia (Helen Morgan, Paul Robeson, Irene Dunne)

Second Film Soundtrack: MGM (Kathryn Grayson, Howard Keel)

Lincoln Center Cast: RCA Victor (Barbara Cook, David Wayne, Constance Towers, John Raitt, William Warfield)

Skyscraper (1965) (SF)

Music by James Van Heusen

Lyrics by Sammy Cahn

Book by Peter Stone, based on the play *Dream Girl* by Elmer Rice

Time: Yesterday

Plot: The heroine dreams herself into romantic entanglements with all the men she meets. A skyscraper is being built next door to her little property and the builders try every means to get her to sell. The matter is concluded when she falls in love with one of the builders.

Cast: 5 females, 11 males

Sets: In and around a small brownstone and a large skyscraper construction in New York City

Choreographer: Michael Kidd

Score includes: "Opposites," "Run for Your Life," "Everybody Has a Right To Be Wrong," "Don't Worry," "I'll Only Miss Her When I Think of Her"

Original Cast Album: Capitol (Julie Harris, Peter L. Marshall, Dick O'Neill, Charles Nelson Reilly, Nancy Cushman, Lesley Stewart)

Song of Norway (1944) (TW)

Music and lyrics by Robert Wright and George Forrest (music adapted from works by Edvard Grieg)

Book by Milton Lazarus, from the play by Homer Curran

Time: Mid-19th century in Norway

Plot: The life of Edvard Grieg.

Cast: 36, plus a corps de ballet

Sets: 7

Choreographer: George Balanchine

Score includes: "The Legend," "Hill of Dreams," "Freddie and His Fiddle," "Now," "Strange Music," "I Love You," "Three Loves"

Studio Recording: (Jones Beach Production) (Walter Cassell, Elaine Malbin, Brenda Lewis, John Reardon, William Olvis)

The Sound of Music (1959) (R&H)

Music by Richard Rodgers

Lyrics by Oscar Hammerstein II

Book by Howard Lindsay and Russel Crouse, suggested by Maria August Trapp's *The Trapp Family Singers*

Time: Early in 1938, Austria

Plot: When a postulant appears to be unprepared for convent life, she is sent to act as governess to the children of Captain von Trapp. The Captain is engaged to marry a woman with whom he quarrels about the Nazis. He falls in love with the postulant, they marry, and the entire family escapes to Switzerland.

Cast: 10 females, 7 males, 7 children

Sets: 13

Choreographer: Joe Layton

Score includes: "The Sound of Music," "My Favorite Things," "Do Re Mi," "Climb Ev'ry Mountain," "You Are Sixteen"

Orchestra: 6 Reeds (no Sax), 3 Horns, 3 Trumpets, 2 Trombones, Tuba, Percussion, Harp, and Strings

Original Cast Album: RCA Victor (Mary Martin, Theodore Bikel)

Film Soundtrack: RCA Victor (Julie Andrews, Christopher Plummer)

Stop the World—I Want To Get Off (1962) (TW)

Music, lyrics, and book by Leslie Bricusse and Anthony Newley

Time: Abstract

Plot: An allegory about life.

Cast: 3 females, 1 male

Set: Unit

Score includes: "Once in a Lifetime," "Gonna Build a Mountain," "What Kind Of Fool Am I?," "I Want To Be Rich"

Original Cast Album: London (Anthony Newley, Anna Quale, Jennifer Baker, Susan Baker)

Sugar (1972) (TW)

Music by Jule Styne

Lyrics by Bob Merrill

Book by Peter Stone, based on the film *Some Like It Hot* by Billy Wilder and I.A.L. Diamond, which was based on a story by Robert Thoeren

Time: 1931, Chicago and Miami

Plot: Two unemployed musicians are witness to a gang murder and are unsuccessfully pursued by the murderers. They join an all-girl band that is leaving immediately for Florida, disguising themselves as girls. One of the boys falls in love with one of the girls. The complexities mount and everything is resolved happily in the end.

Cast: 14 females, 11 males

Score includes: "When You Meet A Girl In Chicago," "Pennyless Bums," "Doin' It For Sugar," "Beautiful Through and Through"

Orchestra: 4 Reeds (including Sax), 1 Horn, 3 Trumpets, 2 Trombones, Harp, Guitar-Banjo, 2 Percussion, Piano-Celeste, and Strings

Original Cast Album: United Artists (Robert Morse, Tony Roberts, Cyril Ritchard, Steve Condos, Elaine Joyce, Alan Kass, Sheila Smith)

Sweet Charity (1966) (TW)

Music by Cy Coleman

Lyrics by Dorothy Fields

Book by Neil Simon, based on a screenplay by Federico Fellini, Tullio Pinelli, and Ennio Flaiano

Time: The present

Plot: Charity is a lady of the evening, works in a dance hall, and always "gives her heart and her earnings to the wrong man." She is tender and funny and Chaplinesque.

Cast: 9 females, 16 males

Sets: 12

Choreographer: Bob Fosse

Score includes: "You Should See Yourself," "Big Spender," "If My Friends Could See Me Now," "Too Many Tomorrows," "Baby Dream Your Dream," "I Love to Cry at Weddings," "Where Am I Going?"

Original Cast Album: Columbia (Gwen Verdon, Helen Gallagher, Thelma Oliver, James Luisi, John McMartin, Arnold Soboloff)

Take Me Along (1959) (TW)

Music and lyrics by Bob Merrill

Book by Joseph Stein and Robert Russell, based on Eugene O'Neill's play *Ah, Wilderness*

Time: Connecticut 1910

Plot: Alcoholic Uncle Sid is courting Lily. Nat (Uncle Sid's brother) has a teenage son, Richard, who writes poetry and reads such scandalous writers as Wilde and Ibsen. Two sets of romances are settled happily.

Cast: 9 females, 11 males

Sets: 6

Choreographer: Onna White

Score includes: "I Would Die," "Staying Young," "I Get Embarrassed," "Take Me Along," "Oh, Please," "Promise Me a Rose," "Nine O'Clock"

Original Cast Album: RCA Victor (Jackie Gleason, Eileen Herlie, Robert Morse, Una Merkel, Walter Pidgeon)

Tenderloin (1960) (TW)

Music by Jerry Bock

Lyrics by Sheldon Harnick

Book by George Abbott and Jerome Weidman, based on the novel by Samuel Hopkins Adams

Time: Late 19th century

Plot: A minister sets out to end corruption with the help of a handsome reporter, a part-time singer. There are double-crosses that help to keep up suspense.

Cast: 9 females, 17 males

Score includes: "Dr. Brock," "Artificial Flowers," "Tommy, Tommy," "The Picture of Happiness," "My Miss Mary"

Original Cast Album: Capitol (Ron Husmann, Eileen Rodgers, Lee Becker, Maurice Evans, Wynne Miller, Eddie Phillips)

Thirteen Daughters (1961) (MTI)

Music, lyrics, and book by Eaton Magoon, Jr.

Time: 19th-century Hawaii

Plot: Although the history of Hawaii is an important element, romance and pageantry figure largely in the production. A father tries to marry off his eldest daughter, so the younger twelve can then marry, in spite of a family curse that decrees *none* shall marry.

Cast: 16 females, 14 males

Sets: 10

Score includes: "House on the Hill," "13 Daughters," "Let-a-Go Your Heart," "Throw a Petal"

Orchestra: 5 Reeds (no Sax), 2 Trumpets, 2 Trombones, 1 Horn, Harp, Guitar, Piano, Violin, Cello, Bass

Original Cast Album: Mahalo (Sylvia Syms, Ed Kenney, Don Ameche, Diana Corto, Monica Boyar)

A Tree Grows in Brooklyn (1951) (SF)

Music by Arthur Schwartz

Lyrics by Dorothy Fields

Book by Betty Smith and George Abbott, based on Miss Smith's novel

Time: Brooklyn around the turn of the century

Plot: Concerns two young people, very much in love, who marry. The husband is a likable ne'er-do-well and the two suffer despite their mutual devotion.

Cast: 9 females, 13 males

Choreographer: Herbert Ross

Score includes: "Make the Man Love Me," "I'm Like a New Broom," "Look Who's Dancing," "Love Is the Reason," "I'll Buy You a Star," "He Had Refinement"

Original Cast Album: Columbia (Johnny Johnston, Dody Heath, Marcia Van Dyke, Shirley Booth)

Two by Two (1970) (R&H)

Music by Richard Rodgers

Lyrics by Martin Charnin

Book by Peter Stone, based on Clifford Odets' play *The Flowering Peach*

Time: The time of the biblical flood

Plot: Noah, his problems with his family, and the uplifting ending when the waters recede.

Cast: 4 females, 4 males (no ensemble)

Sets: 2

Score includes: "Why Me?," "Two by Two," "I Do Not Know a Day I Did Not Love You," "Something, Somewhere," "Ninety Again!," "The Covenant"

Original Cast Album: Columbia (Danny Kaye, Joan Copeland, Madeline Kahn, Walter Willison, Marilyn Cooper)

The Unsinkable Molly Brown (1960) (MTI)

Music and lyrics by Meredith Willson

Book by Richard Morris

Time: Turn of the century

Plot: The triumphs of an indomitable lady from a small American town who seems to have conquered the world.

Cast: 9 females, 25 males

Sets: 15

Choreographer: Peter Gennaro

Score includes: "I Ain't Down Yet," "Belly Up to the Bar, Boys," "I'll Never Say No," "My Own Brass Bed," "If I Knew," "Dolce Far Niente"

Orchestra: 5 Reeds (1 Sax double), 3 Trumpets, 2 Trombones, 3 Horns, Percussion, Strings, Piano

Original Cast Album: Capitol (Tammy Grimes, Cameron Prud'homme, Harve Presnell, Edith Meiser, Jack Harrold, Mitchell Gregg)

Walking Happy (1966) (SF)

Music by James Van Heusen

Lyrics by Sammy Cahn

Book by Roger O. Hirson and Ketti Frings, based on *Hobson's Choice* by Harold Brighouse

Time: 1880, England

Plot: A shoemaker's daughter determines to marry her father's timid apprentice. She makes a master shoemaker of him, as well as a good husband.

Cast: 7 females, 12 males

Score includes: "How D'ya Talk to a Girl?," "If I Be Your Best Chance," "What Makes It Happen?," "Walking Happy," "I Don't Think I'm in Love"

Original Cast Album: Capitol (George Rose, Louise Troy, Norman Wisdom, Sharon Dierking, Gretchen Van Aken)

West Side Story (1957) (MTI)

Music by Leonard Bernstein

Lyrics by Stephen Sondheim

Book by Arthur Laurents, based on a concept of *Romeo and Juliet* by Jerome Robbins

Time: The present in New York City

Plot: A Puerto Rican girl and "white American" boy fall in love. Each belongs to a rival gang. Inadvertently, the boy kills the girl's brother. In the end, he is killed.

Cast: 12 females, 25 males

Sets: 11

Choreographer: Jerome Robbins

Score includes: "Something's Coming," "Maria," "Tonight," "America," "Cool," "One Hand, One Heart," "I Feel Pretty"

Cast Album: Columbia (Larry Kert, Carol Lawrence, Mickey Calin, Ken Le Roy, Chita Rivera, Reri Grist)

What Makes Sammy Run? (1964) (TW)

Music and lyrics by Ervin Drake

Book by Budd Schulberg and Stuart Schulberg, based on the former's novel

Time: The present

Plot: A ruthless and ambitious young man attempts to take over everything from his employer and his daughter. In the end, he loses everything.

Cast: 3 females, 12 males

Sets: 13

Score includes: "My Hometown," "A Tender Spot," "I See Something," "A Room Without Windows," "You're No Good," "The Friendliest Thing"

Original Cast Album: Columbia (Robert Alda, Steve Lawrence, Sally Ann Howes, Bernice Massi)

Where's Charley? (1948) (MTI)

Music and lyrics by Frank Loesser

Book by George Abbott, based on Brandon Thomas' play *Charley's Aunt*

Time: 1892

Plot: Two young ladies are coming to visit Charley and his roommate at their lodgings at Oxford. Charley's aunt from Brazil was to have been there as chaperone but, as she was delayed, Charley has to dress as both his aunt and himself.

Cast: 4 females, 9 males

Sets: 6

Choreographer: George Balanchine

Score includes: "Better Get Out of Here," "My Darling, My Darling," "Make A Miracle," "The Woman in His Room," "Once In Love With Amy"

Orchestra: 5 Reeds (*no* doubles), 3 Trumpets, 1 Trombone, 1 Horn, Percussion, Piano, and Strings

London Cast Album: Monmouth-Evergreen Records (Norman Wisdom)

Whispers on the Wind (1970) (SF)

Music by Lor Crane

Book and lyrics by John B. Kuntz

Time: The present

Plot: Biography of a young Middle Westerner who succeeds in New York.

Cast: 2 females, 3 males

Sets: 1 general set with changing pieces

Score includes: "Whispers on the Wind," "Midwestern Summer," "Neighbors," "It Won't Be Long"

Orchestra: Small combo

Wildcat (1960) (TW)

Music by Cy Coleman

Lyrics by Carolyn Leigh

Book by N. Richard Nash

Time: 1912

Plot: A vigorous woman goes to a small Western city claiming she owns the drilling rights to some land. She hires a staff, actually gets the rights, but finds no oil. As she is about to leave, she hurls a stick of dynamite into a well and unleashes a gusher. Romance also concludes satisfyingly.

Cast: 5 females, 14 males

Sets: 9

Choreographer: Michael Kidd

Score includes: "Hey, Look Me Over," "You've Come Home," "One Day We Dance," "Tall Hope," "You're A Liar"

Original Cast Album: RCA Victor (Lucille Ball, Keith Andes, Paula Stewart, Don Tomkins, Clifford David, Edith King, Al Lanti)

Wish You Were Here (1952) (MTI)

Music and lyrics by Harold Rome

Book by Arthur Kober and Joshua Logan, based on Kober's play *Having Wonderful Time*

Time: Present

Plot: Romances at an adult summer camp.

Cast: 12 females, 16 males

Sets: Action takes place in various locations at Camp Karefree in the Catskill Mountains

Score includes: "Social Director," "Shopping Around," "Could Be," "Where Did the Night Go?," "They Won't Know Me," "Wish You Were Here"

Original Cast Album: RCA Victor (Jack Cassidy, Patricia Marand, Sheila Bond, Sidney Armus, Paul Valentine)

Wonderful Town (1953) (TW)

Music by Leonard Bernstein

Lyrics by Betty Comden and Adolph Green

Book by Joseph Fields and Jerome Chodorov, based on their play *My Sister Eileen* and the stories of Ruth McKenney

Time: The present

Plot: The adventures of two sisters who come to New York City from Columbus, Ohio, in pursuit of careers.

Cast: 5 females, 9 males

Sets: 7

Choreographer: Donald Saddler

Score includes: "Ohio," "One Hundred Easy Ways," "What a Waste," "A Little Bit in Love," "Conversation Piece," "A Quiet Girl," "It's Love"

Original Cast Album: Decca (Rosalind Russell, Edie Adams, George Gaynes, Jordan Bentley, Chris Alexander)

You're a Good Man, Charlie Brown (1967) (TW)

Music, lyrics, and book by Clark Gessner

Based on the comic strip "Peanuts" by Charles M. Schulz

Time: Today

Plot: Cartoon characters inhabiting many and joyous worlds of make-believe.

Cast: 2 females, 4 males (no ensemble)

Sets: One backdrop and a few "blocks" that are moved about and become many things.

Score includes: "Schroeder," "My Blanket and Me," "The Kite," "The Doctor Is In," "The Book Report," "Suppertime," "Happiness"

Orchestra: 5 Reeds (only 1 Sax), 1 Horn, 2 Trumpets, 1 Trombone, Percussion, Piano-Celeste, and Strings (also scored for a small combo)

Original Cast Album: MGM (Bob Balaban, Gary Burghoff, Karen Johnson, Skip Hinnant, Bill Hinnant, Reva Rose)

Zorba (1968) (SF)

Music by John Kander

Lyrics by Fred Ebb

Book by Joseph Stein, based on *Zorba The Greek* by Nikos Kazantzakis

Time: Greece, 1924

Plot: Zorba, a carefree vagabond, talks Nikos into escorting him to claim a legacy (a mine) on Crete. Zorba's romance with an aging Hortense, and Nikos' with a beautiful widow, failure of the mine, and murder are all elements in this musical.

Cast: 12 females, 28 males

Set: One basic set with furniture to indicate various places.

Score includes: "Life Is," "The First Time," "No Boom Boom," "Goodbye Canavaio," "Only Love," "Why Can't I Speak"

Original Cast Album: Capitol (Lorraine Serabian, Herschel Bernardi, John Cunningham, Maria Karnilova, Carmen Alvarez)

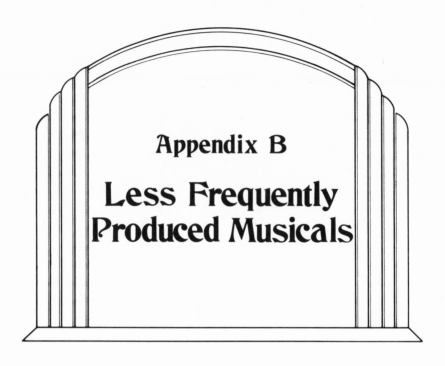

Appendix B
Less Frequently Produced Musicals

THE FOLLOWING LIST, by *company,* contains sketchy information about some shows that are available but not mentioned in the lengthy list in Appendix A. Some of these shows have not reached Broadway. Some are seldom revived. This fact should not prevent the interested producer or musical director from making inquiry about them.

Samuel French Inc.

Alice The Magnificent Music & lyrics by Byron Tinsley. Book by Robert Higgins. A children's play in which Alice is a lion in present-day America.

Alison Wonderland by Thom Racina. A multi-media, TV-oriented Alice.

Curley McDimple (1967) by Mary Boylan and Robert Dahdah. Spoof of Shirley Temple movies. 8 characters.

Cyrano (1973) Operetta. Music and lyrics by Charles George. Book by Jacques Deauville, based on the play by Edmond Rostand. The large-nosed French swordsman, poet, and would-be lover.

The Desert Song (1926) Operetta. Music by Sigmund Romberg. Book and lyrics by Otto Harbach, Oscar Hammerstein II, and Frank Mandel. The Foreign Legion in North Africa.

Donnybrook! (1961) Music and lyrics by Johnny Burke. Book by Robert E. McEnroe, based on the book by Maurice Walsh (from which the film *The Quiet Man* was also made). American prizefighter moves to Ireland, where he was born, and falls in love with a neighbor, but his past catches up with him.

Drat! The Cat! (1965) Music by Milton Schafer. Book and lyrics by Ira Levin. Keystone Kops and a cat burglar.

Fanny, The Frivolous Flapper by Charles George. Amateur lady detective in the Roaring Twenties.

The Fireman's Flame (1937) Music by Richard Lewine. Lyrics by Ted Fetter. Book by John Van Antwerp. 1890s-style melodrama about volunteer firemen.

Frank Merriwell (1971) Music and lyrics by Skip Redwine and Larry Frank. Book by Redwine, Frank, and Heywood Gould. Yale superstar in the early years of this century.

El Grande de Coca-Cola by Ron House, John Neville-Andrews, Alan Sherman, and others. Revue set in Mexican cafe, where the family of the proprietor fill all the roles in an "imported" nightclub show. 5 characters.

Hark! Music by Dan Goggin and Marvin Solley. Book and lyrics by Robert Lorick. Gently irreverent look at growing up in America. 6 characters.

Harrangues by Joseph Walker. Relatively heavy material about black/white relationships.

Heidi Music by Clay Warnick. Lyrics by Carolyn Leigh. Adapted by William Friedberg and Neil Simon from the Johanna Spyri classic—for television.

Inner City (1971) Music by Helen Miller. Lyrics by Eve Merriam. Conceived by Tom O'Horgan. Urban woes illustrated in modern nursery rhymes to a rock score. 9 in cast.

The Last Sweet Days of Isaac (1970). Music by Nancy Ford. Book and lyrics by Gretchen Cryer. Musical satire on a computerized world. 2 characters.

Lend an Ear (1948) Traditional Broadway musical revue, with music, lyrics, and sketches by Charles Gaynor.

Lock Up Your Daughters Music by Laurie Johnson. Lyrics by Lionel Bart. Book by Bernard Miles, based on Henry Fielding's *Rape Upon Rape*.

Man With a Load of Mischief (1966) by John Clifton and Ben Tarver. Intrigue and romance in a roadside inn in 19th-century England. 6 characters.

The Marvelous Misadventures of Sherlock Holmes by Thom Racina. Holmes and the black pearl of the Borgias. Musical mystery for children.

The Merry Widow (1921) Music by Franz Lehar. Book and lyrics by Charles George. European prince woos beautiful American widow.

Minnie's Boys (1970) Music by Larry Grossman. Lyrics by Hal Hackady. Book by Arthur Marx and Robert Fisher. The early days of the Marx Brothers and their indomitable mother.

Mother Earth (1972) Music by Toni Tennille. Sketches and lyrics by Ron Thronson. Depicts the misuse of our environment.

My China Doll by Charles George.

Now (1968) Music and lyrics by Gilbert Martin. Book by Dennis Eliot. One-act teenage musical. Young people learn the need to love everyone.

Now Is the Time for All Good Men (1967) Music by Nancy Ford. Book and lyrics by Gretchen Cryer. Rock musical about a small-town teacher found to be a conscientious objector.

Of Thee I Sing The first musical to win the Pulitzer Prize (1931). Music by George Gershwin. Lyrics by Ira Gershwin. Book by Morrie Ryskind and George S. Kaufman. Running for president with the campaign platform of "Love."

Oh! Susanna Music and lyrics by Ann Ronell. Book by Florence Ryerson and Colin Clements. Based on the songs of Stephen Foster.

Old King Cole Music by Haakon Perderbach. Book and lyrics by Joe E. Grenzeback. The fiddlers three have disappeared.

Orpheus in the Underworld Music by Jacques Offenbach. Book and lyrics by Phil Park. Updated, operetta version of the legend.

Park (1970) Music by Lance Mulcahy. Book and Lyrics by Paul Cherry. A family talks out its problems in a city park. 4 characters.

Peace (1967) Music by Al Carmines. Book and lyrics by Tim Reynolds. Antiwar play based on the works of Aristophanes.

The Pirates of Penzance/The Mikado/H.M.S. Pinafore Operettas by Gilbert and Sullivan.

Robert and Elizabeth Music by Ron Grainer. Book and lyrics by Ronald Millar. The Brownings, husband-and-wife poets of the 19th century.

Seventeen (1951) Music by Walter Kent. Lyrics by Kim Gannon. Book by Sally Benson, based on Booth Tarkington's novel. Teenage love at the turn of the century.

Shelter (1973) Music by Nancy Ford. Book and lyrics by Gretchen Cryer. A television writer lives in an electronic environment. 8 characters.

Show Me Where The Good Times Are (1970) Music by Kenneth Jacobson. Lyrics by Rhoda Roberts. Book by Lee Thuna, based on Moliere's *The Imaginary Invalid.*

Smith (1973) by Matt Dubey, Dean Fuller, and Tony Hendra. A quiet office worker is a secret dreamer.

Streets of New York Music by Richard B. Chodosh. Book by Barry A. Grael, based on the Dion Boucicault play. Gay 90s melodrama about the evil banker and the pure heroine.

The Student Gypsy (1963) by Rick Besoyan, who also wrote *Little Mary Sunshine.* Spoof of grandiloquent operettas.

The Sweetest Girl In Town by Charles George. Love at a summer resort.

Telemachus, Friend by Sally D. Wiener, based on an O. Henry short story. 45-minute song-filled show about an unusual courtship in New Mexico in 1910.

Three To One (1939) (also called *One For the Money, Etc.)* An intimate revue. Music by Morgan Lewis. Sketches and lyrics by Nancy Hamilton.

Three Wishes For Jamie (1952) Music by Ralph Blane. Book and lyrics by Charles O'Neal and Abe Burrows. An Irishman wants a son who speaks Gaelic.

Tom Sawyer by Austin O'Toole. Children's musical version of the Mark Twain classic. 6 characters.

The Vagabond King (1925) Music by Rudolph Friml. Book and lyrics by W. H. Post and Brian Hooker. The operetta in which Francois Villon saves France.

Variety Obit. Music by Mel Marvin. Lyrics by Ron Whyte and Bob Satuloff. The American dream seen through vaudeville sketches and songs. One act. 3 characters.

What's a Nice Country Like You Doing in a State Like This? Music by Cary Hoffman. Lyrics by Ira Gasman. Current political satire. 5 characters.

White Horse Inn (1931) Music by Ralph Benatzky. Book and lyrics by Hans Muller and Erik Charell. Operetta set in an alpine inn.

Music Theater International

Annabelle Broom, The Unhappy Witch by Eleanor and Ray Harder. A children's musical.

Archy and Mehitabel (also called *Shinbone Alley*) (1957) Music by George Kleinsinger. Lyrics by Joe Darion. Book by Joe Darion and Mel Brooks, based on stories of Don Marquis. Archy the cockroach, Mehitibel the cat, and their animal friends in sophisticated New York.

Berlin to Broadway with Kurt Weill (1972) A revue. Music by Kurt Weill. Lyrics by Maxwell Anderson, Ogden Nash, Langston Hughes, Ira Gershwin, Alan Jay Lerner, and others.

Cinderella Music by Jeanne Bargy and Jim Eiler. Book and lyrics by Jim Eiler.

Colette A play with original music by Harvey Schmidt; based on *Earthly Paradise,* the collection of Colette's autobiographical writings by Robert Phelps, adapted by Elinor Jones.

The Drunkard (1970) Turn-of-the-century barroom melodrama. Adapted by Bro Harrod. Music and lyrics by Barry Manilow.

Ernest in Love (1960) Music by Lee Pockriss. Book and lyrics by Anne Croswell, adapted from *The Importance of Being Ernest* by Oscar Wilde.

Jack and the Beanstalk Music by Jeanne Bargy and Jim Eiler. Book and lyrics by Jim Eiler. A children's musical.

Lady Audley's Secret Music by George Goehring. Lyrics by John Kuntz. Book by Douglas Seale.

Oh, Coward! (1972) Words and music by Noel Coward (drawn from a variety of his works). Production devised by Roderick Cook.

O Marry Me (1961) Music by Robert Kessler. Book and lyrics by Lola Pergament, based on *She Stoops to Conquer* by Oliver Goldsmith.

Philemon Music by Harvey Schmidt. Lyrics by Tom Jones.

Pinocchio Music by Jeanne Bargy and Jim Eiler. Book and lyrics by Jim Eiler, based on the book by Carlo Collodi. A musical for children.

Salvation (1969) by Peter Link and C.C. Courtney.

Starting Here, Starting Now Musical revue. Music by David Shire. Lyrics by Richard Maltby, Jr.

The Stingiest Man in Town Music by Fred Spielman. Book and lyrics by Janice Torre, based on Charles Dickens' *A Christmas Carol.*

The Thirteen Clocks Operetta based on James Thurber's *Fantastic Fairy Tale.* Book by Fred Sadoff. Music and lyrics by Mark Bucci and James Thurber.

Tom Sawyer Folk musical for children by Frank Luther, based on the Mark Twain classic.

Triad 3 one-act operas: *Sweet Betsy from Pike, Tale for a Deaf Ear,* and *The Dress,* by Mark Bucci.

The Rodgers and Hammerstein Library

Cinderella (1965) Music by Richard Rodgers. Book and lyrics by Oscar Hammerstein II. Originally written for television.

Gertrude Stein's First Reader (1969) Music by Ann Sternberg. Words and plays by Gertrude Stein. Conceived by Herbert Machiz.

Tams-Witmark Music Library

Around the World in 80 Days (1963) Music by Sammy Fain and Victor Young. Lyrics by Harold Adamson. Book by Sig Herzig, based on the novel by Jules Verne. Adventures of a resourceful Englishman during the winning of a bet which involves going completely around the world. Set in mid-19th century.

Ballad of Baby Doe Opera. Music by Douglas Moore. Libretto by John LaTouche.

Cindy (1964) Music and lyrics by Johnny Brandon. Book by Joe Sauter and Mike Sawyer. Based on an idea by Johnny Brandon and Stuart Wiener. *Cinderella* in modern terms.

The Cradle Will Rock (1937) Opera by Marc Blitzstein. Highly stylized, almost Brechtian, look at labor union activities and the people who live in a troubled factory town.

DuBarry Was a Lady (1939) Music and lyrics by Cole Porter. Book by Herbert Fields and B.G. DeSylva. Men's room attendant dreams he is King Louis XV.

Gift of the Magi Music and lyrics by Richard Adler. Book by Wilson Lehr, based on the O. Henry short story.

Good News (1927) Music by Ray Henderson. Lyrics by B.G. DeSylva and Lew Brown. Book by Laurence Schwab and B.G. DeSylva. College hijinks in the flapper era.

Hit the Deck (1927) Music by Vincent Youmans. Lyrics by Leo Robin and Clifford Grey. Book by Herbert Fields. A waitress follows her sailor sweetheart from Newport to China.

Leave It to Jane (1917) Music by Jerome Kern. Book and lyrics by Guy Bolton and P.G. Wodehouse, based on the play *College Widow* by George Ade. Will the football star play for the rival school?

Love From Judy Music by Hugh Martin. Lyrics by Hugh Martin and Jack Gray. Book by Eric Maschwitz and Jean Webster.

Meet Me in St. Louis Music and lyrics by Hugh Martin and Ralph Blane. Book by Sally Benson, based on the Kensington stories by Sally Benson, and the MGM motion picture (1944). A typical family enjoys the 1904 World's Fair as their daughters fall in love.

The Merry Widow (1921) Operetta. Music by Franz Lehar, based on the London version by Christopher Hassall. Book revisions by Milton Lazarus. New lyrics by Forman Brown. Beautiful American widow is courted by European prince.

Milk and Honey (1961) Music and lyrics by Jerry Herman. Book by Don Appell. American tourists in Israel.

Naughty Marietta (1910) Comic opera. Music by Victor Herbert. Book and lyrics by Rida Johnson Young. Beautiful European emigre meets handsome Ranger captain in 18th-century Louisiana.

The New Moon (1928) Operetta. Music by Sigmund Romberg. Book and lyrics by Oscar Hammerstein II, Frank Mandel, and Laurence Schwab. Just before the French Revolution, a nobleman-turned-revolutionary escapes to New Orleans and finds love.

Oh, Boy! (1917) Music by Jerome Kern. Book and lyrics by Guy Bolton and P.G. Wodehouse. Mistaken identities on a wedding night.

Oh Captain! (1958) Music and lyrics by Jay Livingston and Ray Evans. Book by Al Morgan and Jose Ferrer, based on *The Captain's Paradise* by Alec Coppel. Ship's captain has a wife on each side of the English Channel.

Oh, Kay! (1926) Music by George Gershwin. Lyrics by Ira Gershwin. Book by Guy Bolton and P.G. Wodehouse. Rum-running on Long Island during Prohibition.

Porgy and Bess (1935) Opera. Music by George Gershwin. Lyrics by DuBose Heyward and Ira Gershwin. Libretto by DuBose Heyward, based on the play *Porgy* by Dorothy and DuBose Heyward. Life in a black slum in Charleston, S.C.

The Red Mill (1906) Music by Victor Herbert. Original book and lyrics by Henry Blossom. New book by Milton Lazarus. Additional lyrics by Forman Brown. Musical arrangements by Edward Ward. Two brash Americans find themselves broke in a small town in Holland where they cause trouble but further the cause of romance.

Roberta (1933) Music by Jerome Kern. Book and lyrics by Otto Harbach, adapted from Alice Duer Miller's novel. American football player inherits a dress shop in Paris.

Rose Marie (1924) Music by Rudolf Friml and Herbert Stothart. Book and lyrics by Otto Harbach and Oscar Hammerstein II. Hotel singer loves a mountie, who is framed for murder. Set in Canadian Rockies.

Salad Days (1955) Music by Julian Slade. Book and lyrics by Julian Slade and Dorothy Reynolds. Ingenuous story of young people and their adventures in today's London.

Silk Stockings (1955) Music and lyrics by Cole Porter. Book by George S. Kaufman and Leueen MacGrath, and Abe Burrows. Based on the Garbo movie *Ninotchka* by Melchior Lengyel. American theatrical agent meets Soviet lady officer in Paris and they fall in love.

Sweethearts (1913) Operetta. Music by Victor Herbert. Lyrics by Robert B. Smith. Book by Harry B. Smith and Fred deGresac. The crown princess of Zilania works in a laundry until she can be restored to the throne.

The Vagabond King (1925) Spectacular musical play. Music by Rudolf Friml. Book and lyrics by Brian Hooker, Russell Janney, and W.H. Post. François Villon saves Paris.

The Wizard of Oz Music and lyrics from the 1939 MGM motion picture score by Harold Arlen and E.Y. Harburg. Adapted from the L. Frank Baum book by Frank Gabrielson. Dorothy and Toto meet the Scarecrow, the Tin Woodman, et al., in the wonderful land of Oz.

Appendix C

Published Librettos

The four major rental agencies are not listed here; let it be assumed that you may always "rent" for perusal purposes any libretto (and score) of any musical from the rental agency, usually for just the cost of postage. It is occasionally possible to purchase a script and/or score—certainly from Samuel French—but more often all materials must be returned to the publisher. So this list is mainly provided as a convenience, should you want to own the script, for play-reading purposes.

If a title you seek is *not* listed here, assume that you must contact the pertinent rental agency.

Allegro (*see under* Richard Rodgers).

Anyone Can Whistle, Book by Arthur Laurents, Music and Lyrics by Stephen Sondheim (New York: Leon Amiel, 1976).

Applause, Book by Betty Comden and Adolph Green, Music by

Charles Strouse, Lyrics by Lee Adams (New York: Random House, 1971); *see also under* Stanley Richards: *Great Musicals.*

The Apple Tree, Book by Jerry Bock and Sheldon Harnick, Additional Book Material by Jerome Coopersmith, Music by Jerry Bock, Lyrics by Sheldon Harnick (New York: Random House, 1967).

Baker Street, Book by Jerome Coopersmith, Music and Lyrics by Marian Grudeff and Raymond Jessel (Garden City, N.Y.: Doubleday, 1966).

Bells Are Ringing, Book and Lyrics by Betty Comden and Adolph Green, Music by Jule Styne (New York: Random House, 1957).

Ben Franklin in Paris, Book and Lyrics by Sidney Michaels, Music by Mark Sandrich, Jr. (New York: Random House, 1965).

Brigadoon, Book and Lyrics by Alan Jay Lerner, Music by Frederick Loewe *(see under* Stanley Richards: *Ten Great Musicals).*

Cabaret, Book by Joe Masteroff, Music by John Kander, Lyrics by Fred Ebb *(see under* Stanley Richards: *Great Musicals).*

Camelot, Book and Lyrics by Alan Jay Lerner, Music by Frederick Loewe (New York: Random House, 1961); *see also under* Stanley Richards: *Great Musicals).*

Candide (original production), Book by Lillian Hellman, Music by Leonard Bernstein, Lyrics by Richard Wilbur, Additional Lyrics by John LaTouche and Dorothy Parker, in *The Collected Plays of Lillian Hellman* (Boston: Little, Brown, 1972).

Carnival, Book by Michael Stewart, Music and Lyrics by Bob Merrill (New York: Drama Book Specialists, 1968).

Carousel (see under Richard Rodgers).

Company, Book by George Furth, Music and Lyrics by Stephen Sondheim *(see under* Stanley Richards: *Ten Great Musicals).*

The Education of Hyman Kaplan, Book by Benjamin Bernard Zavin, Music and Lyrics by Paul Nassau and Oscar Brand (Chicago: Dramatic Publishing Co., 1968).

Fanny, Book by S.N. Behrman and Joshua Logan, Music and Lyrics by Harold Rome (New York: Random House, 1955).

The Fantasticks, Book and Lyrics by Tom Jones, Music by Harvey Schmidt (New York: Drama Book Specialists, 1964; Avon Books, 1968).

Fiddler on the Roof, Book by Joseph Stein, Music by Jerry Bock, Lyrics by Sheldon Harnick (New York: Pocket Books, 1971); and in *Best*

Plays of the 60's (Garden City, N.Y.: Doubleday, 1970); *see also under* Stanley Richards: *Ten Great Musicals.*

Finian's Rainbow, Book by E.Y. Harburg and Fred Saidy, Lyrics by E.Y. Harburg, Music by Burton Lane (New York: Random House, 1947).

Fiorello!, Book by Jerome Weidman and George Abbott, Music by Jerry Bock, Lyrics by Sheldon Harnick (New York: Random House, 1960); *see also under* Stanley Richards: *Great Musicals.)*

Follies, Book by James Goldman, Music and Lyrics by Stephen Sondheim (New York: Random House, 1971).

A Funny Thing Happened on the Way to the Forum, Book by Burt Shevelove and Larry Gelbart, Music and Lyrics by Stephen Sondheim (New York: Dodd, Mead, 1963).

Golden Boy, Book by Clifford Odets and William Gibson, Music by Charles Strouse, Lyrics by Lee Adams (New York: Atheneum, 1965).

Goldilocks, Book by Jean Kerr and Walter Kerr, Music by Leroy Anderson, Lyrics by Jean Kerr, Walter Kerr, and Joan Ford (Garden City, N.Y.: Doubleday, 1958).

Grease, Book, Music, and Lyrics by Jim Jacobs and Warren Casey, in *Great Rock Musicals,* ed. Stanley Richards (Briarcliff Manor, N.Y.: Stein and Day, 1978).

Guys and Dolls, Book by Jo Swerling and Abe Burrows, Music and Lyrics by Frank Loesser, in *The Modern Theater,* vol. 4. ed. Eric Bentley (Garden City, N.Y.: Doubleday, 1960).

Gypsy, Book by Arthur Laurents, Music by Jule Styne, Lyrics by Stephen Sondheim (New York: Random House, 1960); *see also under* Stanley Richards: *Ten Great Musicals.*

Hair, Book and Lyrics by Gerome Ragni and James Rado, Music by Galt MacDermot, in *Great Rock Musicals,* ed. Stanley Richards (Briarcliff Manor, N.Y.: Stein and Day, 1978).

Half a Sixpence, Book by Beverley Cross, Music and Lyrics by David Heneker (Chicago: Dramatic Publishing Co., 1967).

Hello, Dolly!, Book by Michael Stewart, Music and Lyrics by Jerry Herman (New York: Drama Book Specialists, 1966).

The King and I (*see under* Richard Rodgers).

Kiss Me, Kate, Book by Bella and Sam Spewack, Music and Lyrics by Cole Porter (*see under* Stanley Richards: *Ten Great Musicals*).

Lady in the Dark, Book by Moss Hart, Music by Kurt Weill, Lyrics by

Ira Gershwin *(see under* Stanley Richards: *Great Musicals).*

A Little Night Music, Book by Hugh Wheeler, Music and Lyrics by Stephen Sondheim *(see under Ten Great Musicals).*

Mame, Book by Jerome Lawrence and Robert E. Lee, Music and Lyrics by Jerry Herman (New York: Random House, 1967).

Man of La Mancha, Book by Dale Wasserman, Music by Mitch Leigh, Lyrics by Joe Darion (New York: Random House, 1966); *see also under* Stanley Richards: *Great Musicals.*

Me and Juliet (see under Richard Rodgers).

The Me Nobody Knows, Book by Stephen M. Joseph (adapted by Robert H. Livingston and Herb Schapiro), Music by Gary William Friedman, Lyrics by Will Holt (New York: Avon, 1969).

My Fair Lady, Book and Lyrics by Alan Jay Lerner, Music by Frederick Loewe (New York: Coward, McCann, 1957).

Of Thee I Sing, Book by George S. Kaufman and Morrie Ryskind, Music by George Gershwin, Lyrics by Ira Gershwin, in *The Pulitzer Prize Plays,* ed. Kathryn Cole and William H. Cordell (New York: Random House, 1940).

Oklahoma! (see under Richard Rodgers).

On a Clear Day You Can See Forever, Book and Lyrics by Alan Jay Lerner, Music by Burton Lane (New York: Random House, 1966).

One Touch of Venus, Book by S.J. Perelman and Ogden Nash, Music by Kurt Weill, Lyrics by Ogden Nash *(see under* Stanley Richards: *Ten Great Musicals).*

Pacific Overtures, Book by John Weidman, Music and Lyrics by Stephen Sondheim (New York: Dodd, Mead, 1977).

Plain and Fancy, Book by Joseph Stein and Will Glickman, Music by Albert Hague, Lyrics by Arnold B. Horwitt (New York: Random House, 1955).

Porgy and Bess, Book by DuBose Heyward, Music by George Gershwin, Lyrics by DuBose Heyward and Ira Gershwin *(see under* Stanley Richards: *Ten Great Musicals).*

Promises, Promises, Book by Neil Simon, Music by Burt Bacharach, Lyrics by Hal David (New York: Random House: 1969).

Stanley Richards, ed., *Ten Great Musicals of the American Theater (Of Thee I Sing, Porgy and Bess, One Touch of Venus, Brigadoon, Kiss Me, Kate, West Side Story, Gypsy, Fiddler on the Roof, 1776, Company)* (Radnor, PA: Chilton, 1973).

_____, *Great Musicals of the American Theater,* vol. 2 (includes *Ap-*

plause, Cabaret, Camelot, Fiorello!, Lady in the Dark, A Little Night Music, Man of La Mancha, Wonderful Town) (Radnor, PA: Chilton, 1976).

Richard Rodgers and Oscar Hammerstein II, *Oklahoma!, Carousel, Allegro, South Pacific, The King and I, Me and Juliet* (New York: Random House, 1955; The Modern Library, 1959).

1776, Book by Peter Stone, Music and Lyrics by Sherman Edwards (New York: Penguin, 1976); and in *Best American Plays 1967–1973*, ed. Clive Barnes (New York: Crown, 1973); *see also under* Stanley Richards: *Ten Great Musicals.*

Sweet Charity, Book by Neil Simon, Music by Cy Coleman, Lyrics by Dorothy Fields (New York: Random House, 1966).

Tenderloin, Book by Jerome Weidman and George Abbott, Music by Jerry Bock, Lyrics by Sheldon Harnick (New York: Random House, 1961).

West Side Story, Book by Arthur Laurents, Music by Leonard Bernstein, Lyrics by Stephen Sondheim (New York: Random House, 1958); *see also under Ten Great Musicals.*

What Makes Sammy Run?, Book by Budd Schulberg and Stuart Schulberg, Music and Lyrics by Ervin Drake (New York: Random House, 1965).

Wonderful Town, Book by Joseph Fields and Jerome Chodorov, Music by Leonard Bernstein, Lyrics by Betty Comden and Adolph Green (New York: Random House, 1953); *see also under* Stanley Richards: *Great Musicals.*

Your Own Thing, Book by Donald Driver, Music and Lyrics by Hal Hester and Danny Apolinar, in *Great Rock Musicals*, ed. Stanley Richards (Briarcliff Manor, N.Y.: Stein and Day, 1978).

You're a Good Man, Charlie Brown, Music, Lyrics, and Adaptation by Clark Gesner (New York: Random House, 1967; Fawcett, 1978).

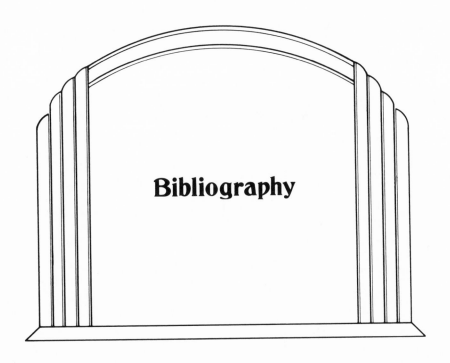

Bibliography

Choreography

Speak to Me, Dance with Me, Agnes deMille (Boston: Popular Library, 1973).

Funding

Performing Arts: The Economic Dilemma, William G. Baumol and William G. Bowen (Cambridge, Mass.: M.I.T. Press, 1968).
The Subsidized Muse; Public Support for the Arts in the United States, Dick Netzer (New York: Cambridge University Press, 1980).
Theatre in America: The Impact of Economic Forces, 1870–1967, Jack Poggi (Ithaca, N.Y.: Cornell University Press, 1968).

Lighting

The Magic of Light, Jean Rosenthal and Lael Wertenbaker (New York: Theater Arts, 1973).

Theater Lighting: An Illustrated Glossary, Albert F.C. Wehlburg (New York: Drama Book Specialists, 1975).

Miscellaneous Reading and History

The American Muscial Theater, rev. ed., Lehman Engel (New York: Collier Books, 1975).

American Vaudeville as Ritual, Albert F. McLean, Jr. (Lexington, Ky.: University of Kentucky Press, 1965).

The Baroque Theater, Margarete Barr-Heinhold (New York: McGraw-Hill, 1967).

Beyond Broadway: The Quest for Permanent Theaters, Julius Novick (New York: Hill & Wang, 1968).

Blacking Up: The Minstrel Show in 19th Century America, Robert C. Toll (New York: Oxford University Press, 1977).

How Theater Happens, Stephen M. Archer (New York: Macmillan, 1977).

The Merry Partners: The Age and Stage of Harrigan and Hart, E.J. Kahn, Jr. (New York: Random House, 1955).

Music and the Art of the Theater, Adolphe Appia (Coral Gables, Fla.: University of Miami Press, 1962).

Musical Comedy: A Story in Pictures, Raymond Mander and Joe Mitchenson (New York: Taplinger, 1970).

On The Art of the Theater, Edward Gordon Craig (New York: Theater Arts Books, 1925).

A Pictorial History of Burlesque, Bernard Sobel (New York: Bonanza Books, 1956).

Theater Backstage from "A" to "Z", Warren C. Lounsbury (Seattle: University of Washington Press, 1968).

Yankee Theater: The Image of America on the Stage, 1825–1850, Francis Hodge (Austin, Tex.: University of Texas Press, 1964).

Words With Music, Lehman Engel (New York: Schirmer Books, 1980).

Music

The American Music Handbook, Christopher Pavlakis (New York: The Free Press, 1974).

Bibliography

The Bacharach and David Song Book (New York: Simon and Schuster, 1971).

The Cabaret, Lisa Appignanesi (New York: Studio Vista, 1976).

Cole, ed. Robert Kimball, biographical essay by Brendan Gill (New York: Holt, Rinehart and Winston, 1971).

The Frank Loesser Song Book (New York: Simon and Schuster, 1971).

Gershwin, His Life and Music, Charles Schwartz (New York: Da Capo, 1979).

Gershwin, Years In Song, (New York: Quadrangle/The New York Times Book Co., 1977).

Great Songs of Broadway (New York: Quadrangle/The New York Times Book Co., 1973).

Great Songs . . . of the Sixties, Milton Okun (New York: Quadrangle/ The New York Times Book Co., 1970).

More Favorite Songs of the Nineties, Paul Charosh and Robert A. Fremont (New York: Dover Publications, 1975).

The Movie Musical from Vitaphone to 42nd Street (as Reported in a Great Fan Magazine) Miles Kreuger, Ed. (New York: Dover Publications, 1975).

100 Best Songs from the 20s and 30s, Introduction by Richard Rodgers (New York: Harmony Books, 1973).

Reminiscing with Sissle and Blake, Robert Kimball and William Bolcom (New York: Viking Press, 1973).

Revue: A Nostalgic Reprise of the Great Broadway Period, rev. Robert Baral (New York Fleet Publishing, 1970).

Ring Bells! Sing Songs! Broadway Musicals of the 1930s, Stanley Green (New Rochelle, N.Y.: Arlington House, 1971).

The Rodgers and Hart Song Book (New York: Simon and Schuster, 1977).

A Selective Musical Collection of the World's Greatest Hits from 1900 to 1919, ed. Aaron Goldmark (Miami Beach, Fla.: Charles Hansen, 1973).

A Selective Musical Collection of the World's Greatest Hits of the Twenties, ed. Ronny Schiff (Miami Beach, Fla.: Charles Hansen, 1972).

Show Songs from The Black Crook to The Red Mill (Original Sheet Music), ed. Stanley Appelbaum (New York: Peter Smith, 1974).

Sir Noel Coward, His Words and Music, (New York: Chappell and Co., 1973).

The Songs of Oscar Hammerstein II (New York: Schirmer Books, 1975).

The Songs of Richard Rodgers (New York: Williamson Music, 1979).

Songs of '76: A Folksinger's History of the Revolution, Oscar Brand (New York: M. Evans and Co., 1972).

Starring Fred Astaire, Stanley Green and Burt Goldblatt (Garden City, N.Y.: Doubleday, 1977).

Stravinsky in Pictures and Documents, Vera Stravinsky and Robert Craft (New York: Simon and Schuster, 1978).

Thou Swell, Thou Witty: The Life and Times of Lorenz Hart, Dorothy Hart (New York: Joan Kahn, 1976).

Town Hall Tonight, Intimate Memories of the Grassroots Days of the American Theater, Harlowe R. Hoyt (Englewood Cliffs, N.J.: Prentice-Hall, 1955).

Treasury of Best Loved Songs (Pleasantville, N.Y.: Reader's Digest, 1972).

The Unpublished Cole Porter, Robert Kimball (New York: Simon and Schuster, 1981).

The Vaudevillians, Bill Smith (New York: Macmillan, 1976).

Producing and Directing

Contradictions: Notes on 26 Years in the Theater, Hal Prince (New York: Dodd, Mead, 1974).

Directors in Action, Bob Thomas (Indianapolis: Bobbs-Merrill, 1973).

Directors on Directing, Toby Cole and Helen K. Chinoy (Indianapolis: Bobbs-Merrill, 1963).

Organization and Management of the Non-Professional Theater, Jim Cavanaugh (New York: Richards Rosen Press, 1973).

Planning and Producing the Musical Show, Lehman Engel (New York: Crown, 1966).

Producers on Producing, Stephen Langley (New York: Drama Book Specialists, 1976).

Producing on Broadway: A Comprehensive Guide, Donald C. Farber (New York: Drama Book Specialists, 1969).

Scenery and Costumes

Broadway and Hollywood Costumes Designed by Irene Sharaff, Irene Sharaff (New York: Van Nostrand Reinhold, 1976).

Designing for the Theater: A Memoir and a Portfolio, Jo Mielzinger (New York: Atheneum, 1965).

The Dramatic Imagination, Robert Edmon Jones (New York, Theater Arts Books, 1941).

220

A History of Costume, Carl Kohler (New York: Dover Publications, 1963).

The Mask of Reality: An Approach to Design for Theater, Irene Corey (New Orleans: Anchorage Press, 1968).

Scenery for the Theater, Harold Burris-Meyer and Edward C. Cole (Boston: Little, Brown, 1972).

Stage Design, Howard Bay (New York: Drama Book Specialists, 1978).

Stage Design Throughout the World Since 1935, ed. Rene Hainaux (New York: Theater Arts Books, 1976).

The Stage Is Set, Lee Simonson (New York: Theater Arts Books, 1963).

The Theater of Robert Edmond Jones, Ralph Pendleton (New York: Columbia University Press, 1977).

Theater Props, Motley (New York: Drama Book Specialists, 1976).

Twentieth-Century Stage Decoration, Volumes I & II, ed. Rene Fuerst and Samuel J. Hume (New York: Arno, 1962).

Sound

Stage Sound, David Collison (New York: Drama Book Specialists, 1976).

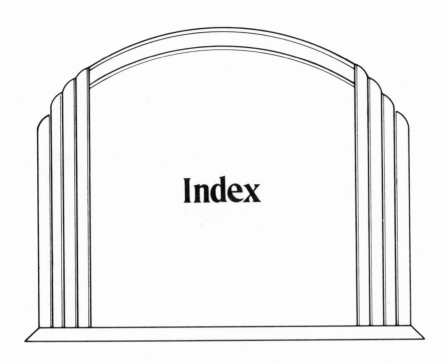

Index

226